For Robin + Marline —
June is just around
the corner —
K + T
xxx

Febrary
2017

LOVE LETTERS TO THE LANDSCAPE

First published in 2016

Copyright © Paul Little Books
www.paullittlebooks.co.nz

A catalogue record for this book is available from the National Library
of New Zealand.

ISBN 978-0-473-30976-3

Paul Little Books
PO Box 78-361
Grey Lynn Auckland
Phone (64) 021 372880
Email pclittle@gmail.com

Designed by Katy Yiakmis
Photography by Stephen Entwisle and others as credited on page229
This photograph by Stephen: the Catlins.

The standard author's royalty for this book is being donated to Forest and Bird

Forest & Bird
GIVING NATURE A VOICE

Printed in China through Asia Pacific Offset Limited

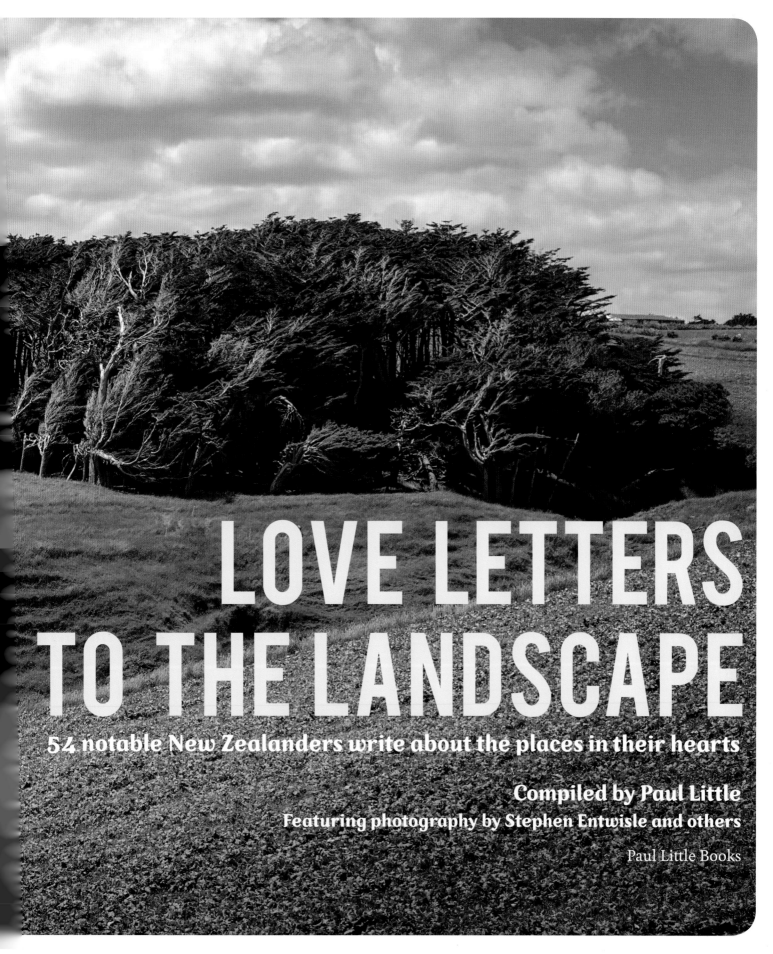

LOVE LETTERS TO THE LANDSCAPE

54 notable New Zealanders write about the places in their hearts

Compiled by Paul Little
Featuring photography by Stephen Entwisle and others

Paul Little Books

Contents

INTRODUCTION

New Zealanders have always had an intensely close bond to their land and landscape. The concept of tūrangawaewae – literally, a place to stand, metaphorically, a place with which one feels connected no matter where in the world you are – is one shared by many. The tangata whenua – the people of the land who were this country's first inhabitants – define themselves by their connection to the landscape in which they live.

As they were encouraged to, the contributors to this book have interpreted the idea of landscape very broadly – from Philip Patston and his suburban deck to Moana Maniapoto and the ocean; from fondly remembered school holiday locations to homes that have been in families for generations; from forests to beaches and hills and everywhere in between.

Kerry Fox's landscape is a road north from Stokes Valley, Brando Yelavich's is a West Coast site he once found after bush bashing for hours, so remote and isolated he doesn't even know its name.

Stacey Morrison's is a place where she has spent only a few hours; Judy Bailey's is the part of Auckland that has been her home for decades.

But for all of them, from Cape Rēinga to Stewart Island, there is a deep emotional bond to the location they have chosen to talk about – a reason why it has earned a place in their hearts.

PAUL LITTLE

Cape Rēinga: the start of a journey.

Stacey Morrison

Cape Rēinga

Mine is a place that I've only been to once and for a short time — but I can't not remember it or how I felt when I was there. I look back on it now like a dawning. I had just got back from Japan where I learnt Japanese by being in that culture. I understood for the first time what you get when you learn a language.

I had grown up in Christchurch and my dad was from the generation that didn't give much thought to learning Māori, so it wasn't part of my upbringing at all. Japan made me realise how important that would be.

I wrote to my grandmother and promised her I would learn Māori, not that she'd ever asked me to, but she was a teacher of Māori.

When I came back to New Zealand, at the age of 18, I got a job on the kids' show *What Now*, based in Dunedin. A lovely man called Peter Hayden was the producer and we were doing something called *From N to Z* which involved travelling from Cape Rēinga to Stewart Island over 25 weekly episodes.

And one of the first things he said to me was: "If we're going to do this, it would be nice if you pronounced Māori words properly." So I had to make the effort.

We started with a blessing at Cape Rēinga and I had no idea what was coming. Having a dawn karakia wasn't something I'd ever experienced or thought of — and now I'm married to Scotty, who is Mr Karakia. I can't imagine it not being part of my own kids' life.

But standing there, I was overcome with emotion. Tears were streaming down my face. I didn't have words for what I was feeling. I couldn't even understand him — but I could feel it and I knew that something had changed. I had started on a journey and there was no going back.

I was so privileged to have that experience as an 18-year-old.

But what a starting point, watching this mass of ocean — the Pacific and the Tasman — come together and you're perched on a skinny strip of land. I can't see how anyone could go there and not be affected by it. It's quite rocky, so you have to make an effort to get there, and I think that's important.

And when you are there, you feel small and at the same time part of something bigger. You feel your place in the world.

I love how we say when we're sending off our dead that this is where they go. I love that you can go there too and see the point from which the spirits leave.

We direct them and talk about how they're going to get through Te Rerenga Wairua. Meanwhile, you feel that at any moment Tangaroa could do whatever he wants with you.

When Mum died, we were in Christchurch. I was working on Māori programmes by then and my friends came down.

> **❝I was overcome with emotion. Tears were streaming down my face. I didn't have words for what I was feeling. I couldn't even understand him — but could feel it and I knew that something had changed. I had started on a journey and there was no going back.❞**

I was struggling about how to do this whole two worlds thing because Mum was Pākehā and we couldn't have her at home like we would have if she had been Māori. I didn't like not having her there.

And a friend said, "She's already gone, darling. She's gone to Te Rerenga Wairua. She's flown away and you don't need to worry about her." This was long after I'd been there and he didn't know I had.

I've listened to Scotty in whaikōrero directing a spirit in how to go — the winds that will take them and where they will go to fly to Hawaiki.

I've never been back to Cape Rēinga but I hope I'd feel more comfortable if I did and not have a repeat of that complicated awakening.

I've seen many people since then struggle with those emotions. At wānanga, when they are learning the language, they will stand up and cry because they can't express their feelings.

We were in Hawaii recently and went to a maungatapu (sacred mountain) they're trying to protect. We stood at the base and the people there explained that the mountain was like their grandmother and what they were doing was like standing in your grandmother's garden and calling out to her to announce you are there. And you do it again at the top to tell her you've arrived.

It was right by a road and people were driving past and staring. They said it was important to do rituals in a public place where people could see, because when they did it changed something in their DNA. It's an awakening for them to realise it happens.

I've seen it with so many Māori, particularly when we do language classes for parents. Sometimes it will take years to answer it, but once it is in you it gnaws away and you have to satisfy it. Cape Rēinga did all those things for me.

Stacey has worked in media for more than half her life, on television both in front of the camera, and behind, and in radio since 1994. Teaming with her husband Scotty Morrison these roles have included reo revitalisation strategies and consultancy for shows such as Whānau Living, Find Me a Māori Bride, Code *and* This Is Piki. *Stacey and Scotty also join forces to teach functional Māori language to parents and whānau within the community group Māori 4 Grown Ups. Stacey was a rangatahi representative in Ngāi Tahu's planning projects in the year 2000 and was one of the authors of NZOA's 'Ngā matakīrea report on Māori mainstream television' 2011, as well as a research project on children's programming for Māori Television in 2013 which introduced Māori versions of shows such as* Dora the Explorer. *She is an ambassador for the New Zealand Breast Cancer Foundation and Water Safety New Zealand.*

Stacey Morrison on assignment in the north.

Coopers Beach: one of many best-kept secrets.

Suzy Cato

Coopers Beach

Growing up in Kaikohe in the 1970s and early 80s we benefited, in so many ways, from living in a small community (3000-3500 people, back then).

My folks knew most of the other families in Kaikohe and most of the other families knew my folks, if not my sister and me — kids were, and often still are, a mere by-product of their parents. The town was small in numbers and small geographically too, so it didn't take too long to walk from one side of it to the other — which we could easily do several times a weekend to catch up with one friend or another.

And because the town was small it was only a short distance to get out past the "Welcome" sign and off to rolling green pastures and beyond; to the many beautiful beaches, dotted along both coastlines.

So many beaches, so many rock-pool

adventures, sand-castle creations and moat excavations. So many waves to jump and tuatua to twist for. So many beaches with endless stretches of sparkly white sand.

One of my favourites would have to be Coopers Beach. Just over an hour's drive from Kaikohe (four from Auckland) it is one of the many best-kept secrets of New Zealand.

With glistening white sand, rock pools at either end and just enough wave to make the jump worthwhile, this beach welcomed us for several wonderful family holidays when I was a nipper, at primary school. We stayed in the same beach house, every trip. It wasn't ours but we grew to love the place.

The house stood behind the row of pōhutukawa that line the edge of the beach. Certainly more of a bach than a house, it was perfect for our family, including grandparents, aunt and cousin who drove up from Hamilton to share the comfy and relaxing sanctuary with us.

> '**We stocked our kitchens with seed heads, leaves, grasses, flowers, gravel and all manner of little non-edible treasures that we would mix into all kinds of culinary creations. Sometimes they were meals, sometimes magical medicines.**'

And it was just a quick trot across the driveway, in bare feet, bucket and spade swinging at our side to the warm sand. The three-metre "dinghy" lay upside down on the grass beneath one of the pōhutukawa and if Dad and Granddad weren't heading out in it to catch dinner, we would sometimes don our salty orange lifejackets to be taken for a tiki tour along the beachline and around the rocks to try our hand at the fine art of fishing.

But fishing was never the great hook for us. That pristine white sand, first thing in the morning, beckoned. The chance to weave patterns with our foot prints and sticks along the magic line where soft, smudgy dry sand meets damp cold wet sand.

We'd fossick for shells, drag seaweed up from the water — popping those delicious little pods with a satisfied squirt, and splash, "swim" and "surf" for hours on end. When I say delicious seaweed pods, I think only of the delight we had finding them and the delicious sound they made as they popped — I only ever tried to eat one, once — blugh! They were far from delicious in taste.

When we'd had our fill of the sun and the tide we'd clamber over, under and around the pōhutukawa. Each became either a castle, a mansion or a humble home. The gnarled roots and branches that draped down low over the cool, shaded sand dividing the space up into rooms — bedrooms, living rooms and, of course, a kitchen.

We stocked our kitchens with seed heads, leaves, grasses, flowers, gravel and all manner of little non-edible treasures that we would mix into all kinds of culinary creations. Sometimes they were meals, sometimes magical medicines.

We'd only tear ourselves away long enough to scamper back across the grass and driveway to brush off enough sand to make it inside for a sandwich and a piece of home baking, and a glass of juice, before heading back down to the beach to continue the adventure.

The first night was always a funny one, as we settled down into the bunk beds of a room we hadn't necessarily been in for some time. The crickets stirring up a racket outside — or inside if someone had left the door open too long. Sleeping bags rustling a little too loudly, the need to pee not strong enough to entice us out the door and along the path to the outhouse.

But, by the next evening, after a feed of fresh fish, or a sausage from the barbie, we would be right at home. Eyes glazing over as we tried to read one of the treasured chapter books from the bach bookshelf.

That bach was another benefit of a small community. It was owned by the principal of one of the schools we attended. Not that we appreciated that fact, when we were just kids. All we knew was that once again we were on holiday at Coopers Beach — and we loved it.

Suzy Cato is a mum of two gorgeous Kiwi kids. As a stay-at-school-working-mum she treasures the time she spends with her kids and loves to traipse up and down the side-line of the soccer field, netball courts, or poolside (something she finds surprisingly enjoyable since she was allergic to sports herself, as a nipper). When she's not with her kids, Suzy can be found making radio and video for them and their friends, with the help of her husband. To find out more about what she's up to visit www.suzy.co.nz.

Suzy Cato: so many beaches.

Ōmāpere's dunes: sandy landmark.

Anika Moa

Ōmāpere

Mum and Dad had broken up before I was two years old. He was a gypsy at heart and one day he just left. He was married to a woman in Amsterdam for a while. He was in and out of bands and prison from around the time I was born until one day when I was 13 and he made contact.

I was walking home from school in Christchurch when this green, Hori-as car pulled up, driven by a guy who looked like Bob Marley. He wound down the window and said, "I'm your father."

"Sweet," I said, and I jumped in and we went to a party.

He flew my brother and me up to Auckland and we all got stoned under the Harbour Bridge — at least, my brother and Dad did. It was the first time I'd smoked pot, and it didn't work for me.

At one point my mum said I couldn't see "that man" any more but we talked her around, and my brother and I spent six weeks with him that year.

Then he moved down to Christchurch and that's

when the actual relationship began. He finally made the effort to be a father. He came to every single one of my sports games, and every music performance I did.

I didn't call him my dad. I called him my mate.

Once, he took us up north to Ōpononi and Ōmāpere, to stay with my Uncle Rata. We went out on my uncle's boat. We crawled over the rocks and caught crabs. We went swimming at the beach. I learnt to love the ocean.

It was the first time I'd met anyone who said, "Oh, I'm your uncle," and took me and treated me like a niece. It was an amazing feeling. And that was the start of my relationship with those places.

My family are originally from Pawarenga, which is 45 minutes from Kohukohu, across the harbour from Ōmāpere.

> **'It was the first time I'd met anyone who said, "Oh, I'm your uncle," and took me and treated me like a niece. It was an amazing feeling. And that was the start of my relationship with those places. '**

Ralph Hotere was born at Mitimiti, which is near there, and we are related to him because my mum married his nephew. I never met Ralph, because he lived in Dunedin, but for my second album he said I could use anything of his that I wanted to for the cover, but I couldn't find anything suitable.

After that first visit north with Dad, every year for the next five years he took us to travel all around the Hokianga — Kohukohu, Mitimiti, Ōmāpere.

He wasn't just a northern person. He lived everywhere.

He was born in Auckland but grew up in Pawarenga and Kaitāia.

Because he was a musician he travelled and played in every pub and town around. When we had him in our lives, from when I was 13 until I was 27, he would literally sing for our supper.

He certainly wasn't rich. But he had his car, and we cruised from place to place, with him performing wherever we stopped. And we always had a dog or cat in the car with us — something we had picked up along the way. Dad loved to collect strays.

We met random people and stayed at their houses. They were always great, but I was too young to realise how lucky I was to meet them.

And we met musicians, like Herbs, but I didn't appreciate that either. I'd be thinking about missing my mum instead of enjoying what was going on around me.

I always think of Dad when I'm in the Hokianga — it's the association between the place and him that makes it extra special to me.

I'm not sure why I think of Ōmāpere as my special part of the Hokianga. I just feel a very strong bond with it. It's not just the beach, or just the dunes, it's the whole picture.

It was inevitable that when I got married I would go back there, and we had our wedding at the Copthorne Hotel in Ōmāpere. A lot of the kids who work there are my family — four cousins and an aunty and I love how the menu never seems to change.

I still go there once a year even though I don't know my Hokianga family that well any more. After Dad died, in 2007, when he was 51 and I was 27, contact with the Māori side of the family got less and less and I didn't know how to reconnect with them.

Perhaps I'm starting to reconnect. I did a video clip called "Falling in Love Again" there, which was hilarious. A lot of cousins turned out for that. I am an extrovert and I still love meeting family members.

Dad is buried in Pawarenga. I feel he's travelling with me whenever I leave Auckland and drive north. I think about the stories of the spirits walking along the beach, getting to Cape Rēinga and jumping off. I believe that. It may seem foolish, but it's this daughter's belief that her dad did that and I feel it every time I walk along the beach.

Ōmāpere is not my home — that will always be Christchurch, which is a place I love — but it's my spiritual home. I'm not especially religious but Ōmāpere brings out something spiritual in me. I can feel something there. I think it's the presence of someone I loved. It may not be "real" real, but it's real in my mind.

Anika Rose Moa is a clever, charismatic and funny as all hell singer songwriter from New Zealand/Aotearoa. She began writing pop songs at the tender age of 13 and is now an established singer, writer and mother of three. Back in 1999 Anika was spotted by Atlantic Records and became the youngest Kiwi artist to be signed to a major American record company. She recorded her debut album 'Thinking Room' in the Big Apple. Back in New Zealand the album ricocheted to number one and her stellar career began. Anika was living the dream, but terribly homesick so she returned to focus on her burgeoning success here. Anika has a long list of accolades to her name and while she's terribly humble, here's a few: APRA Children's Song of the Year 2014; Best Children's Album — 2014 New Zealand Music Awards; Best Female Solo artist — 2010 New Zealand Music Awards.

Anika Moa expressed her appreciation.

Dame Gillian Whitehead

Ruakākā

It's the fifties. My parents have bought, for a few hundred pounds, an acre of land high above the Ruakākā river. It's a wilderness — mānuka, acacia, thistles, agapanthus, cape gooseberries, plum and peach trees, tall sheltering tacoma hedges. There's a tiny two-roomed bach, an army hut where my sister Joyce and I share a very uncomfortable double bed, a cookhouse, a long-drop out the back. We love it, and spend much of the summer there, reading in the shade of mānuka and mingimingi, eating plums and cape gooseberries, looking out over the river and the estuary to the sea and the mountains and islands engraved forever on my mind's eye — Manaia, the Hen and Chickens, Sail Rock, Little Barrier. My father builds a track down the steep cliff to the Deep Hole, which is perfect for swimming. My parents buy a clinker-built dinghy, and the estuary and the river become our playground. We walk over ranges of hot sandhills (not a building in sight) to swim in the ocean, our family often enough alone on the beach — no flags, no lifesavers. We know where the parore shelter under the shade of a gnarled, semi-submerged pōhutukawa, where to find the sea slugs in a lagoon near the river mouth. We take the dinghy up river, traveling with the spring tides, under the bridge with no sides where once a cow fell in the river, and even as far as the second bridge. We gather firewood and in the evening after tea play statues and hide-and-seek with the children next door until it's too dark to see, and every year gather firewood and ferry family and friends across the river to savour half-burnt half-raw sausages and baked potatoes around a bonfire. And when it rains, we play canasta with the kids next door, or read an ancient *Boys' Own Paper* annual; I also have access to our neighbours' extensive Agatha Christie collection.

So many birds. Sea birds, land birds, swamp birds, river birds. Oystercatchers are new in the area. We watch fairy terns out by the ocean, and at night against the distant roar of the sea hear bitterns and moreporks, watching the double sweep of a lighthouse out at sea and marvelling at the brightness of the stars.

It's the seventies, early eighties. I've been living in London and Europe for nine years before I return for the first time, drawn back in part by images of the headland and islands under

Ruakākā: a 1970s photo of Dame Gillian's sister walking through sandhills that are now a suburb.

a cloudless sky. My parents have built a retirement house, or rather, built a spacious concrete basement with a thirties house, brought down from Whangārei, atop it. There was a misunderstanding. When they asked for the site to be cleared, they meant the building site, but somehow the whole section was razed, and the wilderness destroyed; there's a tame kikuyu grass-covered section in its place.

My father has a large and thriving vegetable garden, sheltered by bamboo, which to my eye looks charmingly South-East Asian. On my first visit, after nine years of European perspective, I find the hills alarmingly exaggerated, and the horizon tips up at the edges — everything looks so much closer, so much clearer. Over the next seven years I make occasional visits first from Europe, later from Sydney. My first opera, *Tristan and Iseult,* is to be performed in the Auckland Festival, and, to get away from pre-rehearsal nerves, I take the dinghy up the river and feel perfectly happy and relaxed. The bach, now a single room, for a short time becomes my studio, where I write *Low Tide, Aramoana,* a piece setting Cilla McQueen's poem of the same name, presaging the 20 years I'd be based on the Otago peninsula, but also a farewell to the Ruakākā estuary. We have learnt that my father has cancer; the house is sold; my parents will move to Auckland. I toy with the idea of buying the place, but decide it's all too difficult.

> **So many birds. Sea birds, land birds, swampbirds, riverbirds. Oystercatchers are new in the area. We watch fairy terns out by the ocean, and at night against the distant roar of the sea hear bitterns and moreporks, watching the double sweep of a lighthouse out at sea and marvelling at the brightness of the stars.**

It's 2014, perhaps 60 years since our parents first bought Ruakākā. I'm living on the Otago peninsula, settled in another landscape I love. Joyce, who's travelling in Northland, sends me an email. Our old place is for sale for a few hundred thousand dollars. It takes me all of 30 seconds to decide to put my Sydney flat on the market, and somehow, through good luck and a buoyant Sydney property market, a few months later the three of us are living in Ruakākā again — I'm upstairs, Joyce and Ian downstairs.

Ruakākā is much changed, as you'd expect in 60 years. Once we stayed on the edge of a small contained settlement served by a gravel road, now it has joined up with other small settlements — Marsden Point, One Tree Point, Takahiwai — and spread over the sandhills, with new roads and sub-divisions continually opening up. Most of the houses are modest — there is little ostentatious wealth here.

The house has been let over the years, and is in need of renovation. The old gold carpet has been ripped up and the matai floorboards repaired and polished, the walls painted — the house scrubs up well. By next summer, we hope to do up the old bach as a studio cum library cum sleep-out.

There is a small lemon orchard, and other fruit trees — feijoas, grapefruit, mandarins. There are still plums, and we've planted cape gooseberries. Over 35 years, the bamboo had become a forest, metres deep, along the cliff. Scrub cutter and mulcher are dealing to it; most of it has gone now and we can see the islands again — Marotere, Taranga, Sail Rock, Hauturu-o-toi. Why should we always call them by their European names? Once we've got through the bamboo we'll try to rebuild the track, buy a dinghy and row up the river again, and be able to swim without driving to a beach.

The estuary is a bird sanctuary now, where exhausted oystercatchers rest after storms at sea. But the swamp is drained and there are no bitterns, mynahs are the incomers. But morepork still call; in winter, seven spoonbills roost in the pōhutukawa by the water, and herons croak as they follow the course of the river.

It feels like the completion of a circle, being back where I was so happy as a child. It just feels right, my tūrangawaewae. It smells right, the weather patterns are familiar, the days lengthen and shorten at the right tempo — in the south, the change is almost perceptible on a daily basis, always too fast.

And so much remains the same; it's very satisfying to see other children swimming in the Deep Hole, exploring the estuary by kayak or paddleboard, owning the landscape as we once did. Sometimes you can see the sweep of a lighthouse beam, but the lights of tankers waiting to enter port usually obscure them.

I've seen many changes in Ruakākā over 60 years, knowing it in the fifties, the seventies and today, and wonder how it will continue to evolve as more and more people are driven north and south of Auckland. For sure there will be more and more subdivisions. In the meantime, it will see me out. The play of light on the ocean, the changing patterns of clouds at sunrise and sunset and the ebb and flow of the tide will continue to delight whoever is lucky enough to be here.

And I still marvel at the brightness of the stars.

Born and educated in New Zealand, Gillian Whitehead, after studying in Britain with Peter Maxwell Davies, worked as a free-lance composer in Europe and Australia before returning to New Zealand. A steady stream of works over the years has established her as one of the major composers working in the Australasian region. Her music has been widely performed and broadcast, with many pieces recorded or released on disc. Her works include operas and monodramas, pieces for orchestra, choir and other large ensembles as well as numerous chamber, choral, and solo works, pieces with directed improvisational content and pieces involving taonga puoro. In 2000 she was honoured by the Arts Foundation of New Zealand as one of their five inaugural laureates, awarded for artistic achievement. Three times the winner of New Zealand's SOUNZ Contemporary Award, she received an honorary doctorate from Victoria University in 2003, the CANZ Citation for services to New Zealand music in 2007 and in 2008 the DCNZM for services to music.

Gillian Whitehead (centre) with her mother and sister in the stern and aunt in the bow on a dinghy on the Ruakākā river in the 1950s.

Tinopai Bay: the Smith family bach.

Diane Foreman

Tinopai Bay

Tinopai Bay in the Kaipara is the site of my partner Jason's family bach, built by his grandparents about 100 years ago. It was far-seeing of them to build it back then, and it's wonderful that they've passed it down through the generations.

In fact, it's where his parents met, because both their parents had baches there. It's a quintessential piece of New Zealand. I have houses all over the world but this is the place where I feel most at peace.

I love it because it's particularly tidal. You sit on the old deck, which seems to be hanging on by two fingernails, and watch the tide come in and out, and there's something magical about that. To me it's symbolic of life itself, the ebb and flow of the cycle of good and bad. I could watch the tide forever.

There are baches on either side but none of them is particularly beautiful. The family bach is set high up. There is a road between it and the beach, but it's designed so you can't see the road from the building.

I've only been going there for the past seven years. I hadn't even been to the west coast before that, so I didn't know the area at all. Then I met Jason, who farms there. The bach is half an hour from his farm. It's not flash, it's classic. It's boats and rocks, kids and grass and pōhutukawa trees.

The house itself is just a little two-bedroom weatherboard building. One bedroom is a bunk room. There's a small kitchen and a bathroom that's been added on at the back.

It's full of the sort of things that you think about when you're away from New Zealand. Even when I'm in my London home, my thoughts often drift back to that deck on the Kaipara Harbour.

But it is also full of a family history that's been accumulated over the years. Family is very much part of the experience.

From a big family tree there's one branch of cousins near, another branch across the road, and hordes of them from another branch in several baches across the bay. If someone goes fishing they will bring you a snapper or some oysters.

There's also a strong link with my own childhood, when my grandparents had a bach at Kawakawa Bay. That's the site of some of my best early memoires — playing on the rocks and around the boatshed, potato chips and spiders with Fanta and ice cream.

But when I was about seven my family moved to Australia. Where we were, there was no bach. We went to Perth, which is as far as you can go from anywhere without ending up in the ocean. My father came from there, and it doesn't have a bach culture. It's just big open beaches stretching away on either side.

And when we moved back to New Zealand in my teens, the old family bach here had been sold.

I didn't experience that bach feeling again until I met Jason and his family. And it's related to the fact that I deal with property and move in and out of places a lot.

> **'For me, being a well-rounded person means being able to sit cross-legged on the grass at Tinopai and eat your barbeque off a plastic plate.'**

Tinopai resonates with my past and makes my past and my present seem very much the same. After all the things that have happened over 55 years, I'm back where I started — sitting on a beach. I didn't know how much I'd missed it. When I was married to my previous husband, we had yachts. I loved that but when you sail you're always somewhere different. Being on or in the water is not the same as watching it.

Until recently, I was constantly moving, visiting new markets and looking at new opportunities for my company. Now I'm quasi-retired and live part time in London and have a home in Remuera.

So I haven't had and don't have a lot of permanence in my life when it comes to property. And I'm adopted, so I don't have the sense of generational pull that Jason does. When I came to Tinopai first I responded to that sense of family, the sense of people who had been doing the same thing for years.

I have a house at Ōmaha but that's a very different experience. It's Trelise Cooper's old house, and it's very beautiful and very designed and has the heated swimming pool. And I love it, but not for any sense of it being a special place in New Zealand. The sort of experience you have at Ōmaha is the same experience you can get in the USA or Italy.

For me, being a well-rounded person means being able to sit cross-legged on the grass at Tinopai and eat your barbeque off a plastic plate.

But that doesn't mean the next day I can't go to Ōmaha and have a dinner party and get in the pool. I think what makes being a New Zealander great is that you're just as comfortable in either situation. When I travel, I notice that New Zealanders can fit in most societies and that's because we're very grounded.

The reality is I probably only get to Tinopai three or four times a year, but that only makes it more special. Because Jason lives in the Kaipara and I live in Auckland, Ōmaha has become the place where we each meet halfway.

So going further north to the bach is a special occasion.

We have friends who come over from Australia for the summer and the one thing they want to do more than anything is have lunch on the deck at the bach.

Diane Foreman CNZM, is chairman of Emerald Group. She was named New Zealand Entrepreneur of the Year 2009 and was a World Entrepreneur of the Year judge in 2010. Diane is a patron of New Zealand Entrepreneurial Winning Women, author of In the Arena *published in 2015 and was named as one of the 50 most powerful women in Asia by* Forbes *magazine in 2014. The retired ice-cream maker is a mother of four and grandmother of five.*

Diane Foreman enjoys the view from the Tinopai bach.

Huapai: the Lynch family home as it is today.

Suzanne Lynch

Huapai

My place is Huapai, where we lived when I was a girl. Now it's like a suburb of Auckland, but back then it was a really rural town. We used to go into Auckland just once a year to do the Christmas shopping.

We had a poultry farm with 2000 chickens, which was a lot in those days. They were all free range or on soft litter. It was pretty chaotic. It was my job to feed the wheat to the ones out in the paddocks every night after school. We traded eggs for groceries at the local store.

It was a magic time in my life. I had every pet animal under the sun. My oldest memory is when Mum took me to the zoo because my pet lamb had died and I was absolutely distraught. We went to the children's zoo and there was a South African mountain-climbing goat. I couldn't leave this goat alone, and the goat couldn't leave me.

The keeper came up and said: "You really like that goat, don't you?"

"I love this goat," I said, "and this goat loves me. Could I take her home. How much is she?"

"How much have you got?"

My mother was quietly having a fit, and I opened up my purse and said I had ninepence.

"Would you believe it?" he said. "That's exactly what the goat costs."

I gave him the money and we got the goat in the back of the car and a few months later it had twins. It used to climb up on the chicken house and wait for me to come home from school.

They got added to all these other waifs and strays I looked after.

I had a chicken with a broken leg that I put plaster of Paris on and used to call Hoppity because she hopped everywhere and would follow me to the ends of the earth. We had a dog called Sylvester who howled at the moon, and three or four cats who all had kittens.

If the local sheep farmer found an orphaned lamb he would come and ask if I could mind it and feed it up for him. I rode my horse Smoky to our tiny country school.

It was a wonderful way to grow up. Life was really real in those days. Those four acres of land were my anchor. And to this day, when I'm out in the country I get the feeling of being back on that little farm.

I was looking at doing a teaching job in China, and I went over there and there was not one blade of grass in sight so in the end I said no because I couldn't have handled that.

Another great thing about living in the country was that you felt so safe. We roamed over every inch of the countryside playing with the other kids. And they all came to our place because we had the bracken hut. We stayed out every day until it was dark.

My mother wrote and typed out copies of a neighbourhood newsletter — called *The Cackler* because of the poultry — which was passed around the households. (By the way, the connection between The Chicks' name and the poultry farm was purely co-incidental.)

Music was part of life too. Kevin Borich of the La De Das was our next door neighbour. His family had an orchard there. We even recorded something when I was eight, my sister Judy was 10 and he was 11. We did it at Mascot Studios and they told us to come back when we were a bit older.

> **❝I had a chicken with a broken leg that I put plaster of Paris on and used to call Hoppity because she hopped everywhere and would follow me to the ends of the earth. We had a dog called Sylvester who howled at the moon, and three or four cats who all had kittens.❞**

We kept up to date with music and entertainment. We had the first TV in the neighbourhood and people would come over to our place to watch the likes of Cliff Richard. Sometimes we would all go to the Boriches for a sing-along and everyone brought a plate.

We left Huapai when I was intermediate-school age. I cried my eyes out. I was absolutely distraught. My happy place in my mind, even today, is still that little farm.

I found the goats a home with a lady who had goats. The pet lambs had turned into six fat sheep and the new people promised they'd keep them there but I'm not so sure that happened.

I wanted to be a vet, but my mother told me I was far too small and I would have to be a secretary.

I drove out there a couple of months ago to see the old homestead. The acorn I planted is now a big tree. The house's owners have done it up beautifully and my dream is to one day buy it back.

We moved to Henderson first and we seem to have always been lucky with musical neighbours because one day we saw the great guitarist Peter Posa was playing on our neighbour's deck, so we asked for his autograph.

He said he'd give it to us if we sang him a song so we did.

And his manager, Ron Dalton, took our number down on the back of a cigarette packet.

I was very excited and went home and told my mother.

"You won't hear from him again," she laughed. "Now dry the dishes."

Two weeks later Ron Dalton rang with a song for us —"The Hucklebuck". He took us out shopping for clothes, sorted out our image and that was it — we were launched.

My knees were knocking so hard I could hardly stand up when we did our first TV show but there was no turning back. It was an amazing time.

And our parents were totally supportive of us. I look at 14-year-old kids I teach now and wonder how our parents could have let us do it. When we started touring our mother came as chaperone — we were only 14 and 16 — and everyone looked out for us. I had so many big brothers in the business and we're all still very close.

Suzanne Lynch established a name in New Zealand in the popular 1960s duo The Chicks with her sister Judy, performing on the television show C'mon *and later as a solo performer on* Happen Inn. *She spent the major part of the 1970s living and working in England, as a session singer, working on albums with Chris De Burgh, Art Garfunkel, Showaddywaddy, Cleo Laine, and The Walker Bros. She sang on a live recording with Neil Sedaka at the Royal Festival Hall, with the London Symphony Orchestra, and toured England with Neil. In 1974, she joined Cat Stevens' band, singing on three albums, and touring the world twice with him. Back in New Zealand Suzanne has been the television vocal coach on all series of* New Zealand Idol, Stars In Their Eyes, *and* New Zealand's Got Talent *shows. She teaches contemporary vocal technique and performance, performs both solo, and with The Ladykillers vocal group, whose members include Jackie Clarke, Tina Cross and their special guest, Annie Crummer.*

Suzanne at home with *that* goat.

Wendyl Nissen

Kawau Island

I have had many love affairs with coastal parts of New Zealand. I'm a sucker for a pretty bay with white sand and clear blue water, of which there are many in this country. It doesn't take much for me to fall over in a heap of longing and gratitude especially if there is a pōhutukawa tree under which I can fall.

My first love was a little bay at the entrance to North Harbour on Kawau Island where I spent a decade of my formative years on holiday with my family.

In the 70s it was common for families to have a bach where they spent school holidays with the kids, and for the Nissens it was a rented bach in Barkers Bay, Kawau Island.

Getting there was a nightmare by today's standards but back then it was just, well, how you went on holiday. First there was the long two-hour drive to Sandspit, north of Warkworth from Auckland. Then we would pile all our food and luggage into our boat which was moored there and head out past the spit, into the Hauraki Gulf and over to the island. A trip I remember as being so long there was nothing to do but curl up and go to sleep — my avoidance tactic which works to this day.

Our boats varied over the years from a 12-foot clinker dinghy with a Seagull outboard towing a Sabot yacht my father had built to a rather flash Hartley launch. My cat Pizza came every time and would howl from her spot in the bow.

Kawau Island: the jetty at Barkers Bay.

Sometimes, and I remember these times vividly, we would break down half way there. Usually in bad weather with night approaching. We would all sit in silence drifting out to sea on the current as my father battled with the motor to get it going. And usually he would, or some kind boatie would tow us to the island.

There were only four baches in the bay, one was ours, the other was rented by our friends and the others were used by their owners. So it was a close community of four families and anything from 10 to 20 kids depending on visitors.

> 'Our mothers sat under the huge pōhutukawa tree which dominated the bay where they smoked, played Scrabble or cards and indulged in "elevenses" which stretched out through the afternoon well into the evening.'

Most meals were shared up on the hill at the barbecue site where parents quaffed wine and children played guitars and sang folk songs . . . hard to imagine these days, but hey, it was the 70s.

During the day we sailed our Laser yachts around the island, or joined our dads fishing or diving, or simply walked through the bush to the other side of the island where there was a huge sandy bay for body surfing.

Our mothers sat under the huge pōhutukawa tree which dominated the bay where they smoked, played Scrabble or cards and indulged in "elevenses" which stretched out through the afternoon well into the evening.

No one seemed too concerned about what we got up to, as long as we turned up by nightfall.

At night, wallabies, introduced by Governor Grey, would hop about the bay in abundance and you could hear weka and kiwi in the bush.

Our bach was a very simple affair. Long-drop toilet with a double seat in the garden, water tank full of mosquito larvae out the back, two bedrooms and a bunk room for my brother.

Hydrangeas grew in abundance, washing was done in an old wringer and I have no idea how my parents fed us.

We were two fast-growing teenagers yet somehow my mother managed to take all the food for our six-week summer holiday in one lot.

As I grew into a teenager I worked out many of life's new difficulties in that bay. There were older girls who taught me how to shave my legs and get rid of bikini hair. We all competed to see who could get the best tan and wear the coolest bikini — mine was string, just saying.

I had a morbid fear of sailing out too far in case I capsized, so my friend Fiona took me out and made me capsize the boat over and over until I could right it and keep going no worries. My first lesson about feeling the fear and doing it anyway.

And then there was the drinking. Upset that my parents wouldn't let me join my boyfriend on the mainland for New Year's Eve, I somehow found a bottle of gin and emptied it into me. This was achieved during the boat trip over to Mansion House where the best New Year's party was had in those days. I have little memory of that party and somehow the rest of the kids found me, bundled me back into the dinghy and deposited me in my bedroom without waking my parents. Which was rather a waste of time as a few hours later I was vomiting copiously out of my bedroom window.

My mother's horror and disgust the next day was not so much that I had poisoned myself but that the whole bay heard me vomiting. There were standards, even in the 70s. To this day I have a wary relationship with gin.

I had my first romance at the age of 12 with a boy I met at the Bon Accord Harbour yacht club. We would sail out into the harbour to meet each other, or his parents would come to pick me up on their launch for a day out. Like most holiday romances, the next year we had both moved on.

I graduated from catching sprats off the jetty to hauling in snapper by the bucket loads to scuba diving for scallops and crayfish with my dad.

And then it was over. I was 18 and was living in town with the boyfriend whose absence brought on the gin overdose. Our friends in the other bach were no longer our friends and my parents moved on to buy their own bit of land by the sea on the mainland.

I've never been back to Kawau and probably never will. When I think of that decade I remember picture perfect summers, tanned legs smothered in baby oil, the jolt of the sail as you go about, the reassuring tug on the hook from a snapper and the angst of teenage years soothed by friendship. I like those memories just as they are and don't want to risk damaging them with a reunion.

Wendyl Nissen is a writer, editor and broadcaster. Her books include Domestic Goddess on a Budget *and* Wendyl's Home Companion. *She is editor of the New Zealand edition of* The Australian Women's Weekly.

Wendyl Nissen (right) with friends and Pepper the poodle.

Stony Batter: historic gun placement on Waiheke Island.

Penny Whiting

Stony Batter

Stony Batter Historic Reserve, at the eastern end of Waiheke Island, is named for its unusual rocky outcrops and is the site of extensive tunnels and gun emplacements dating back to WWII. For many years my kids and I would spend school holidays on this amazing farm and piece of New Zealand.

My daughter, Erin, had a love of horses and my son, Carl, also enjoyed them, even if it was to get to where the young boys and dogs could hunt for pigs on the property. The property owner was John Spencer and his farm manager, Bumpy, and I would help about eight kids saddle up horses for a day of exploring, riding, hunting and fishing.

My daughter learnt to ride here and all her early riding was done on the property.

We all rode lots of horses and ponies and eventually, about 20 years ago now, when Bumpy wanted to move back to Gisborne, we rode all the horses from Stony Batter to Gisborne. First we took them on a barge to Kawakawa. There was Bumpy and me and eight kids, aged between about eight and 13, and we rode them down SH2 — along the beaches of Whakatāne and around the East Cape and finally to Gisborne. It was a wonderful adventure that took us a month, sleeping in paddocks along the way.

> **'Bumpy would pick us up from the ferry in the farm truck and once we got over the mound and to the first hill and saw the Waiheke Channel and the view out to Pakatoa it was an indescribable feeling.'**

There's nothing quite like riding a horse up to the McDonald's drive-through and asking for 15 burgers.

We had one support vehicle — a truck with hard feed in it for the horses. Some days I went ahead in the truck and if I saw a nice-looking farm I'd knock on the door and introduce myself and say: "We've got eight kids and these horses. If we can sleep in your paddock I promise we'll leave it better than we found it." And they were always positive about letting us sleep there.

The kids were used to the outdoors from all the holidays we'd had at Stony Batter. We were living in Herne Bay but we loved getting out there whenever we could.

Bumpy would pick us up from the ferry in the farm truck and once we got over the mound and to the first hill and saw the Waiheke Channel and the view out to Pakatoa it was an indescribable feeling.

In summer I took my boat down and anchored it out and the girls, riding bareback, would swim the horses out to it. For any onlookers it was a startling sight.

At times the kids were needed to help in the yards as the merino sheep needed many hands while drenching or clipping their nails. But as the stockyards were just next to the Stony Batter tunnels the helpers were not with us for long, as this labyrinth of musty tunnels was very exciting and soon drew them away.

One notable feature was a mound we used to have to drive over getting in and out of the property. On one occasion we had found that one of the animals had been butchered and all that was left was the head, legs, tail and a bit of the guts.

So the mound was put in place to make it harder for them to get access to the stock. Unfortunately, it also made it harder for us to get the car in and out, especially in winter. But that was what lay behind the story of the road being blocked off.

This is a magnificent landscape. Unlike much of the rest of Waiheke, which has gone through a property boom, this place hasn't changed at all over the years. Views all around the Hauraki Gulf and surrounding area always made me feel I was flying or gliding over the hills while checking stock in the truck or from the quad bike. The views are breathtaking and of course are all about the sea and coastline that I love. I enjoyed looking into the bays, at the translucent waters and contours of the coastline. I had a bird's eye view of the coves and anchorages.

Penny Whiting and co on the trail.

My own childhood holidays were spent on the boat with my father at Hooks Bay on the north-east tip of Waiheke, just down from Stony Batter, so I've always known it well. We would take the little dinghy in and walk up the same hills.

I think there may even be another family connection going back some time. The story is that my grandfather was stationed there during World War II, manning those gun emplacements where my kids would play so much later.

Penny Whiting has been fortunate to have been sailing and boating all her life, first as a toddler racing with her father, D'Arcy, in the Hauraki Gulf, as a teenager doing more serious racing and as a young woman tackling lots of water-based sports. Her sailing school is 50 years old this year. She managed to fit the teaching of adults aboard the family yacht in the early days as well as lots of surfing in New Zealand and overseas. Her father took Penny and her brother Paul on several ocean races when they were in their teens. She received an MBE for services to sailing in 1990. Penny married at 30 to Doc Williams and they have two great children, Carl, a double world champion in sailing and jujitsu, and Erin, who is a professional horse rider and coach for show jumping. These days she enjoys all the grandchildren and manages to get away boating each New Zealand winter.

Thorne Bay: start of the golden weather.

Nathan Haines

Thorne Bay

That magical stretch of coastline from the Hauraki End of Takapuna beach to Milford is something very special to me. I was born in Takapuna Hospital and grew up in Beachhaven. And in the 1970s, my mother would take us down to Takapuna beach in the school holidays.

We'd bundle into her Fiat 500 with our polystyrene surfboard sticking out of the roll-back roof and head to the beach. We'd explore around the rocks at low tide, sticking our fingers into unlucky sea anemones, and clamber under rock shelves looking for big crabs.

I started playing for the New Zealand Youth Orchestra when I was nine. We had our first tour to Australia in 1982 and I went busking to raise money. The first place I did it was outside the butcher's in Takapuna shops. That shop has gone but the feeling of those shops is still the same. It's not like the other side of the harbour. Whenever I come back over the bridge to this side I breathe a sigh of relief. It still feels like it did when I was growing up — but with more traffic.

We had an amazing childhood of roaming for

> **'We'd bundle into her Fiat 500 with our polystyrene surfboard sticking out of the roll-back roof and head to the beach. We'd explore around the rocks at low tide, sticking our fingers into unlucky sea anemones, and clamber under rock shelves looking for big crabs.'**

kilometres doing the things kids used to do then — riding our bikes for miles and having adventures in the bush.

As a teenager I'd visit Thorne Bay accessed from Minehaha Avenue with my older mates — they called it "The Mediterranean" — and dive off the rocks at high tide, trying to impress girls.

I left New Zealand in 1991 and the thing I got most homesick for — particularly in winter, when it was summer back in New Zealand — was the beach. And the more time I spent away the more important it became, especially because London has no beach. You can go to Cornwall with its amazing coastline but the water is cold and it takes five hours to get there. You can get to Spain from London in that time.

I am absolutely an all-year-round water person. Sometimes, coming back to New Zealand for shows in winter, I would go swimming if it was one of those beautiful sunny winter Auckland days. In the northern hemisphere that wouldn't happen because there is no warmth in the sun.

After my first 10-year stint in London I returned to New Zealand during a mid-winter tour. It was one of those incredible fine spells, and I headed to Thorne Bay for a swim, not caring about the cold water and only wishing to cleanse away the London grime.

In the shade of an ancient pōhutukawa sat an old block of flats with a "To Let" sign in the window . . . and so began a three-year stint back in New Zealand, living happily sequestered in a 1960s bach with my girlfriend (now wife Jaimie) overlooking Thorne Bay. I wrote albums, swum on most days, and we partied into the night and watched the sun rise over the Waitematā.

We eventually moved back to London but with the arrival of our first child, Zoot Webster Haines at the very end of 2014, thoughts once again turned back to New Zealand. The pull of the ocean, the lifestyle and of course family was too intense to ignore.

Nathan Haines and son Zoot.

We now live in Hauraki overlooking the Harbour Bridge, Auckland City and the ever shifting eco-system of the mangroves at Shoal Bay, but we're still only a quick walk to Takapuna Beach. Running about with Zoot and Jaimie and swimming in the Waitematā under the gaze of Rangitoto, I feel a wonderful completeness. More than 40 years ago as a young boy I loved Takapuna Beach, and now as a father and husband I love it even more.

Nathan Haines is one of New Zealand's most successful and respected jazz musicians. His first solo album was released in 1994, and the ensuing 20 plus years have seen him record and perform all over the world. Nathan is a headline artist at London's Ronnie Scott's Jazz Club, and he's performed at many international festivals and clubs as both a solo artist and also as a DJ. Nathan has won New Zealand's Tui Jazz Album of the Year award three times. Nathan now lives in Auckland with his wife Jaimie and son Zoot Haines.

Judy Bailey

Birkenhead Point

When I was asked to write a piece about a part of the New Zealand landscape that is special to me I immediately thought about the spectacular eastern Coromandel Peninsula, a stretch of glistening bays and white sandy beaches, fringed by pōhutukawa and echoing to the sounds of tūī and fantails.

I thought too, about the rolling, golden hills of the Māniototo in Central Otago, or the primal West Coast beech forests.

We live in paradise and we are indeed spoilt for choice. Because of that it can be easy to overlook the very real beauty to be found right on our doorstep.

My doorstep is Birkenhead Point.

It nestles on the northern slopes of Auckland's Waitematā Harbour, an unpretentious, North Shore suburb of our largest city. The western side of the point looks out across the harbour to the purple-hued, bush-clad hills of the Waitākere Ranges. Beyond the ranges lie the wild, west coast beaches and the turbulent waters of the Tasman Ocean. From time to time, fierce storms roll in over the ranges, whipping the generally tranquil waters of the inner harbour into a frenzy of white caps and pitching yachts. Commuter ferries bustle to and fro, connecting the point to the skyscrapers of downtown Auckland.

The prevailing westerly brings cooling breezes in the summer and chilly gusts in winter. And it's from the west too, that we are gifted those glorious sunsets. I'm often to be found spellbound on our verandah, gazing at the spectacular evening light shows as the sun sinks below the horizon and the world turns pink, then orange, then red before darkness falls. Then the lights of the Te Atatū Peninsula and beyond twinkle like so many diamonds in the velvety night.

The eastern side of the point has a commanding view of the city and the Harbour Bridge. The safe haven of Little Shoal Bay lies at its foot, with Northcote Point rolling down to its eastern arm. A small boat yard dominates the western side of the bay, and all winter it's a hive of activity as boaties beaver away at the barnacles, readying their craft for the season ahead. It's a sure sign summer's on the way when they're all finally craned into the welcoming waters of the bay.

The open green fields that bound the bay to the north are a favourite family picnic spot, not to mention a great venue for outdoor movies, Christmas carols, cricket and touch.

There's a playground alive with children year round and the recent addition of a series of exercise stations for adults means you can now work out and enjoy the glorious view at the same time.

Part of Birkenhead's charm is the real sense of history you find here.

In the 1700s it was seafood that first drew Māori to the spot. The area around Birkenhead Point was famous for its sharks, so much so that canoes from as far away as Thames would come to fish the waters here. The first European settlers arrived in 1857. They'd come expecting to find open farmland, but instead were confronted by an unforgiving wilderness, the like of which they'd never encountered. They had to struggle for every inch of arable land. Then in the 1870s an enterprising farmer found that the teatree covered land was perfect for fruit growing, particularly for strawberries. It became the fruit bowl of the North Shore.

> **'I'm often to be found spellbound on our verandah, gazing at the spectacular evening light shows as the sun sinks below the horizon and the world turns pink, then orange, then red before darkness falls.'**

In fact in the early 1900s it became quite the thing to make special ferry trips across from the city to the Birkenhead Wharf at the foot of Hinemoa Street for afternoon teas of strawberries and cake.

Originally called Woodside, the name Birkenhead was apparently adopted because the little settlement was a ferry ride away from the city centre and was developing along a series of ridges . . . very like its namesake in England, where people were ferried across the Mersey to the city of Liverpool.

The Victorian, coral-coloured, Chelsea Sugar Refinery dominates Chelsea Bay, to the west of the Point. Chelsea's dams and rolling parklands are a haven for birds and dog walkers and hikers. From here you can walk through the bush along the coast line and drop down into Kendall's Bay, a secluded little sandy cove that can only be reached on foot.

Building on the refinery began in 1883 on the wilderness of what was then Duck Creek. Of course the workers had to have somewhere to live and many of the sturdier refinery homes remain today. The manager's brick house still stands behind the refinery, as do four semi-detached, two-up two-down homes that housed the most skilled workers. Surrounded by towering oaks and plane trees, they are a slice of old England in the world's biggest Polynesian city. Clydesdale horses played a big part in the life of the refinery, hauling huge loads of raw sugar from the ships to the store sheds up the hill.

Any parade in Birkenhead today includes a team of Clydesdales in a nod to the important role they had in the history of the village. Through the early part of last century Birkenhead was very much a sugarworks town. Life revolved around the refinery. Now, thanks to some fierce lobbying by active locals, its old horse paddocks have been turned into parkland, Auckland's voracious appetite for more housing kept, for the moment, at bay.

There's history too, to be seen on the streets. Many of the old kauri villas are protected. Some of the best are to be found on the broad sweep of Hinemoa Street as it curves elegantly down to the wharf.

It is though, without a doubt, the abundance of bush and parkland that makes this place special. And for me, one of the real jewels of Birkenhead Point is Le Roy's Bush, a 12-hectare block of native forest you can immerse yourself in, in the heart of the city. It runs from the ridge of Onewa Road down through the valley and ends in the raupō wetland that adjoins Little Shoal Bay. The bush was originally bought by a visionary Auckland sailmaker, Edward Le Roy in 1918. Le Roy happened to be a keen gardener and an enthusiastic collector of plants, many of which he transplanted from his brother's home on Great Barrier Island. Among them, towering kauri, tōtara, rimu and pōhutukawa. During the great Depression of the 1930s he earned the loyalty and respect of his canvas workers by refusing to lay them off. Instead he set them to work creating tracks and seating so his bush could be enjoyed by everyone.

We owe him a huge debt of gratitude. The bush is an oasis of calm, a haven from the roar of the city, echoing only to the sound of the native birds, tūī, fantails, kererū and grey warblers or riroriro. So much birdsong. Le Roy's has been enjoyed by generations of families. My own children played here as they were growing up, damming the stream, climbing the rocks beside the waterfall, building forts in the raupō and huts in the trees. They were able to live the lives of country children and yet have all the benefits of being in the middle of the city.

I was moved to write about Birkenhead Point because I was out walking the dogs one evening in early summer. It was balmy, there was a warm breeze, just enough to stir the air, the harbour was a sparkling bright blue. Tūī sang and chased each other through the shining leaves of the pūriri. The heat of the day shimmered off the footpath. Fat wood pigeons perched precariously on the power lines, seagulls swirled in a cloudless sky, pink doves cooed. It was, I thought, a perfect moment, the sort of day that makes you happy to be alive, and in that moment I really saw the beauty that surrounds me, beauty I had taken pretty much for granted all these years.

Judy Bailey is a writer and broadcaster living in Auckland. She fronted prime-time news for 26 years, becoming one of the most recognised faces in New Zealand. On leaving TVNZ she fronted Māori Television's ANZAC Day programme for nine years and has been involved in a number of documentaries and television series. Judy has long been an advocate for children. She is a founding member, trustee and presenter for the Brainwave Trust, an organisation that brings the latest research in neuroscience to those who work with children and young families. She is also a patron of the Muscular Dystrophy Association, The National Collective of Women's Refuges and the North Shore Hospice. In 2010 she was created an officer of the New Zealand Order of Merit for her services to broadcasting and the community. She is married to the managing director of South Pacific Pictures, producer and director Chris Bailey. They have three children and five grandchildren.

Judy Bailey at home in Le Roy's Bush.

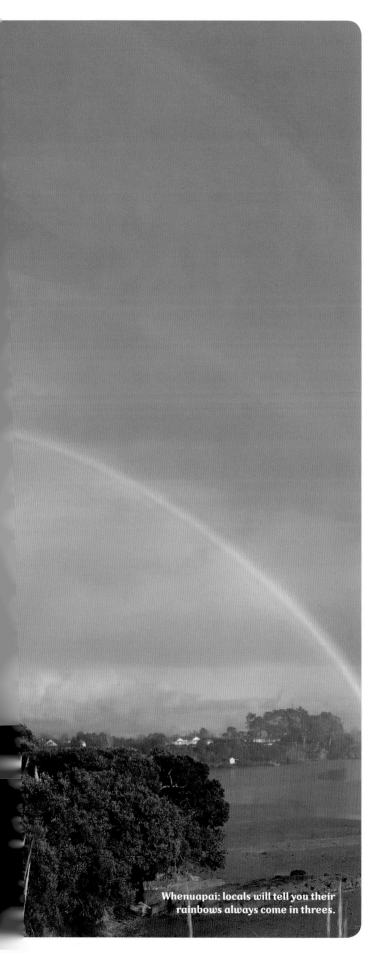

Whenuapai: locals will tell you their
rainbows always come in threes.

Suzanne McFadden

Whenuapai

Here, in Whenuapai, the phenomenon
of things swooping down from the sky
towards our little village is nothing out of
the blue.

With an Air Force base on the back
doorstep, it's normal to see (and feel) a
big-bellied Hercules rumbling across your
car roof as your paths intersect, or watch a
swarm of parachutes drifting down to earth.
Being buzzed by a kereru, drunk on pūriri
berries, is an everyday hazard.

It has the very best sunsets. Red, orange,
pink, gold, charcoal and blue; streaked,
feathered, blazing; reflected off the serene
water. And sometimes, there are triple
rainbows.

But the tornado that descended from
our sky unannounced in the summer of
2012 was a different matter. And it changed
a lot of things that day in the place we call
The Pai.

For one, it messed with the landscape.
Bouncing off village landmarks as it went,
the lethal whirlwind slayed 90-year-old
radiata pines, knocking the grand old
gentlemen off their shallow-rooted feet, and
bowed huge Norfolk pines at their waists.

No one in the village saw it coming that
Thursday lunchtime, a few weeks before
Christmas. A friend who was driving across
the Auckland Harbour Bridge saw it — not
the spinning funnel cloud you'd imagine
from *Twister*, but more a massive flying
carpet of dark, dirty air, menacing its way
west along the harbour.

It was one of those hot, still, moody
days, that now make me anxious. A
thunderstorm warning had been issued,

with a footnote advising to bring your pets inside. I flippantly posted on Facebook that I'd ensure Ernie and Bert, our goldfish, were safe and sound.

I was writing at my desk in my home office when it arrived. The air which had been strangely static and electric, was suddenly moving fast. I watched a torn-off tree branch whip past my window one way, and seconds later, fly back again. I vaguely remember the roar . . . crouched down in my hallway in the middle of the house, pretty certain the fish and I would be whisked away like Dorothy and Toto.

> **'The air which had been strangely static and electric, was suddenly moving fast. I watched a torn-off tree branch whip past my window one way, and seconds later, fly back again. I vaguely remember the roar.'**

But the house and I stayed put. In minutes the storm had passed, but it dropped down long enough to wreak havoc on our village. Concrete power poles were toppled like dominos, landing skilfully in the street. Barbeques and Pink Batts hung from those overhead lines and trees still standing; people who didn't have a trampoline before, now had two. All that remained of a neighbour's aluminium garage was the door handle (they never found the rest).

The damage, though, was to things. No people were hurt in Whenuapai, and somehow, mercifully, it sidestepped our primary school.

But in the neighbouring suburb of Hobsonville Point, where the tornado had continued its ruinous path, the news was tragic. Three men were killed on the building site of the new secondary school where my youngest son now goes.

Another thing the tempest changed that day was a community's spirit. For the next three days, residents — and people from outside the village — banded together. Armed with chainsaws, axes, rakes and utes, they went from house to house cleaning up the damage, helping people they may have never spoken to before.

There were gaping holes left in our landscape, but the village had knitted closer together. And it had only intensified my love for this place where I lived.

I moved here 18 years ago with my seven-year-old son. Having grown up on a farm in Wellsford to the north, I'd wanted us to get further from the fast encroaching city, but still be in Auckland. That's when I accidentally discovered Whenuapai Village on a Sunday drive.

Tucked in behind the Air Force base, which has been there for 80 years, the village hugs the upper reaches of the Waitematā Harbour. All roads in pass by tilled rows of red soil (Whenuapai translates from Māori as "good land") and lush green pasture. Well, for now anyway.

It isn't always beautiful. It's tidal, and when the water heads back to Auckland city, there is a lot of grey, gluggy mud and only a few metres of sand. This past summer, it smelled bad too. When the long, hot days baked the mud at low tide, the stench of broiled hermit crabs lingered.

We are blessed with marine life. Maybe I shouldn't reveal how, in certain months of the year, we can wheel a dinghy down to the river, row out 100 metres, throw out a line and haul in (very legal) snapper for lunch. Kids have even caught inquisitive kingfish in their arms on the water's edge.

Pods of dolphins — who also know about the fish — come visiting too. There's a phone tree, where neighbours ring each other and simply say, "They're back". The odd Bryde's whale, orca or decent-sized shark will often lose their way and cruise to the head of the harbour. I even saw a squadron of pelicans once.

In summer, the river is busier than the village roads, filled with kayaks, paddleboards, dinghies, fizz boats and show-off jet skis. On still mornings, you can clearly hear the coxswains calling their commands as school rowing crews scull back from Riverhead. And in the evening the happy sound of revelling office parties on board the old wooden ferries travels across the water.

When I got married, staying here wasn't even a matter for negotiation. It's been a great place to raise our two boys. The eldest rode his bike to school across the Air Base runway — before 9/11 changed that. The kids muck about in little boats, play spontaneous mass soccer matches in the park, and come home when it's dark and they're hungry.

Now The Pai is about to undergo another, this time massive, change. We always knew the fields couldn't stay green forever. Our rural seaside village with no more than 500 homes is about to expand — 9000 new houses, they say; 8000 more jobs. The city has finally caught up to us.

You can't stop a tornado; you can't stand in the way of progress. But we'll still have our sunsets and our rainbows.

Suzanne McFadden is an author and freelance journalist who specialises in capturing the essence of people. Over three decades, she has written in both national and international media, initially making her name covering sport for the New Zealand Herald. *She became internationally renowned for her coverage of the America's Cup between 1995 and 2003. Suzanne has thrived on the freelance writing life since 2001, broadening her scope to include human interest features for some of the country's leading magazines. She was voted Qantas Sports Feature Writer of the Year two years running, and is also a two-time winner at the New Zealand Magazine Media Awards. Her first book,* Striking Gold, *published in 2016, is the story of New Zealand hockey's remarkable victory at the 1976 Montreal Olympics. Suzanne is married to journalist Eugene Bingham, and they have two sons, Marc and Kieran. She loves having her own slice of the Pai.*

Suzanne McFadden takes to the local waters for some fishing.

Big King: once there were three.

Denys Watkins

Big King

Big King is situated at the top of Mount Eden Road. Take a right at the top, before you reach the vacuum cleaner mart. I've been taking the blue heeler here for eight years. She's ready to go at 3.30 or 4. They have an inbuilt clock and respond to regimented procedures.

I'm not sure if the dog is taking me or I'm taking her. It's a reciprocal activity, keeping us both from the black dog and the spectre of bodily expansion.

We begin at the ball-throwing, small field, with five minutes of intense retrieving. Blue heelers need to have a job and after two and a half years they are not interested in social interaction with other dogs.

These cones used to be Three Kings. The area is still known as this, including on bus signage. But the truth is there is only one volcanic cone, as the other two have been ground down as a quarry, creating a large hole in the landscape.

Things that previously existed here had exotic descriptions, such as Scoria Cones, Tuff Cones, Explosion Pits, Horseshoe Rings, Dykes and Flows, Tuff, Scoria and Lapilli Beds. This was before the major quarrying invasion, around 1927.

It is early June, 4 o'clock in the afternoon. The sun is about a metre from the top of the Waitākeres — that is, from where I'm standing on the upper concourse or field. This field has no practical purpose, it is possibly simply a walkway. These small flats roll and curve adding animation to the long diagonal shadows cast from the pōhutukawa and pūriri that bisect the uneven field. Thirty years ago this was a scrub and privet-covered non-event. The planting — native and exotic with the occasional fruit tree — adds texture, pattern and density.

Though not Samarkand or Kew, the scale and physicality, variation of light from east to west make this a haven and great walk on which to percolate ideas and solve problems from a day's studio activity.

The banks are planted with spaces between the trees. The only fruiting at this time of year is the magenta berry and flower on the pūriri. This is food for kererū. I've not seen them here, but around October tūī are in full command. On the higher field flocks of eastern rosella swoop and zoom around the base of the cone.

> 'This is food for kererū. I've not seen them here, but around October tūī are in full command. On the higher field flocks of eastern rosella swoop and zoom around the base of the cone.'

The cone rises at the end of the field. You can walk straight up from here or take the more pastoral route, winding around the bottom with a good workout on the stairs to the next level.

The cone is crowned with a beautiful concrete water tank. Its purpose, though not obvious, could be interpreted as a landing pad for extraterrestrial objects. It's surrounded by kūmara pits and middens, the remnant of a previous encampment. This cylindrical water tank, monumental in proportion, holds court, sending messages to other water tanks in the isthmus. From here you can observe the rainclouds drifting slowly across from New Lynn and Avondale. You have eight to 10 minutes to make it down the mountain without getting soaked.

Local kids from the state houses in the cul de sacs surrounding the cone play a defiant game, picturing and tagging the water tank. After two to three days the council park employees paint it out in green or grey, and the cycle begins again. I'm not a great fan of public sculpture, but these industrial monuments of practicality hold my interest.

A large water pipe sits suspended midway down the hill, two metres or so in circumference and painted an army green, spanning a distance of approximately 40 to 50 metres. This pipe is a perfect sculptural complement in scale and size to the water tank on the top. It has proved to be a popular activity for children to take on its challenge with a degree of apprehension, depending on their level of fearlessness and challenge. My own granddaughters used to find this the best part of this activity after the Friday school pickup.

Along with using the ball thrower for the dogs. One of them engaged in the selective activity of collecting squaresided stones — that is till high school loomed on the horizon. The large hole that was recently the quarry, is now home to 15 yellow CAT earthmoving machines, ploughing and shoving large amounts of soil to partially fill the cavernous wound so that highrise apartments can be constructed in this hole in the ground. This activity could be seen as architecturally progressive, bearing some resemblance to the phenomenon known as EARTH art in the early 1970s (primarily in America) but that's stretching credibility. What outcome this will have for the sanctuary, for walkers and dog owners is precarious.

I hope that this small park, a promenade between dog owners and pastoral flaneurs, will continue. I have engaged in this "round the cone activity" nearly every day for eight years, Christmas and Easter included. I've come to appreciate changing seasons and the possibility that my universe is contained within a small plot of pastoral pleasure, one where I can socialise with the psychologist, marine biologist, sail maker, social worker and groundkeeper, not excluding the dogs whose exercise and curiosity is relative to that of the humans.

Denys Watkins was born in Wellington in 1945 and lives in Mount Eden, Auckland. He studied at the Wellington School of Design, the Central School of Art & Design and the Royal College of Art in London. He was a senior lecturer at the Elam School of Fine Arts, University of Auckland from 1980 to 2011. A practising artist, he works mainly in painting and drawing, also print assemblage, ceramics and photography. His work is held in public and private collections in New Zealand and overseas.

Denys Watkins and the dog who takes him to Big King.

Grey Lynn Park: skateboards, swings and shadows on the skyline.

Joel Little

Grey Lynn Park

We moved into our house in Dryden Street, Grey Lynn, in the year hmmmm . . . I think I was seven and my sister was five, so it must have been 1990 I guess. All I remember clearly is realising that directly across the road was what looked like a never-ending expanse of green, which in my mind offered up endless possibilities for adventures, and I felt like we'd come to the right place.

Once Mum taught us how to cross the road properly (she made us walk two driveways down before we crossed in order to put some distance between us and the cars that sometimes came flying over the hill), I spent pretty much every minute I could for the rest of my childhood in that park, throwing my schoolbag in the front door after school and charging over there for as many hours as possible until it was too dark to see anything anymore.

That park quickly became the centrepiece for a lot of what I now consider to be some of the bigger moments of my life growing up.

There weren't a lot of electronic distractions for us kids (back in myyyyy day) and the park seemed to serve as a babysitter of sorts for parents in the area, in that there was never a shortage of similarly aged people to play with. I made quick close friends with a lot of the neighbourhood kids, some of who I still see around sometimes, and I know they remember spending their afternoons and weekends at that park as well as I do, because we still talk about it.

I made one or two enemies down at that park too, and it was always an interesting time when we ran into each other, but I don't remember ever telling my parents about any of the bigger problems we had. After a while it felt a little like that park became its own separate world and us kids would figure out how to deal with any issues we had in our own way while we were there.

There were the big life events — when I was eight years old my Nana was outraged when she found out I still couldn't ride a bike, so she marched me and my bike over to the basketball court and taught me on the spot. From then on, racing my bike around every corner of the park became a daily event as we searched out all the steepest sections of hillside to speed down, crossing off the tamer slopes and noting our favourites for future visits. Eventually it got to the point where I knew how many pedals it would take to get me up each hill and how many it would take going back down to get my speed to a point before I'd get too scared and have to squeeze the brakes. Over the years, as the council started putting in new pathways, we spent days figuring out the most fun way to cover every path and take each corner in the quickest and most efficient way possible.

> **'I spent pretty much every minute I could for the rest of my childhood in that park, throwing my schoolbag in the front door after school and charging over there for as many hours as possible until it was too dark to see anything anymore.'**

I remember really appreciating Guy Fawkes for the first time, watching all the neighbourhood families spread out around the park, putting on their mini displays and thinking how magical it all was, and in our younger years running around the next day collecting used fireworks up in plastic bags, taking them home and taping them together like guns, then running back down and battling each other with them while they were still spilling out black powder. Then, when we were a little older, in the days when you could still get sky rockets, we'd run around shooting at each other with Moon Travelers (which were tiny little sky rockets). I remember watching a friend of mine holding one between his teeth and lighting it and thinking he was a complete idiot and my hero at the same time.

In the winter my friends and I would walk home from Kowhai Intermediate in the rain and do big diving slides through the giant puddles on the league fields. In the summer I'd play basketball for hours with my best friend, Linden, who lived three doors up. He was way better than me, and the very rare occasions when I'd manage to beat him would put me in a good mood for days.

Summer at the park also involved watching touch rugby tournaments and kilikiti and volleyball through our living room window and being unable to control the urge to grab a ball or bike or something to take down there because everyone else was having so much fun and we were missing out.

Then there were the tougher times, like the day I borrowed the skateboard my sister had got from The Warehouse and tried to drop in on the skateboard ramp twice, bailed both times, cried (told everyone to shut up 'cos I wasn't crying), and decided never to skate again.

There were also the many nights going through my "I'm going to be a big time soccer player" phase, where I'd head down to the park every afternoon and wouldn't come home until I'd juggled that damn ball a minimum 200 times in a row without it hitting the ground. This was a dark period for me.

Then of course there was the annual Grey Lynn Festival, the biggest day of the year for that park and always an exciting time for us kids, waking up and seeing all the cars and trucks and stalls and stages that had magically appeared since we left the previous evening. We'd head over there and without fail run into at least five or six good friends within the first half an hour, and this seems to be one of the traits of the festival that holds true to this day. You're also guaranteed to come across three or four old friends you haven't seen in a long time, seven or eight old acquaintances you hoped you'd never run into again, and at least nine or 10 dudes with BO and juggling sticks.

I lived across from that park for 14 years. Grey Lynn has definitely changed a lot now. Mum has moved out of our house, houses cost a couple dollars more than they used to, and the Foodtown at the Grey Lynn shops is a Countdown . . . but every time I go back there is still something about that park that just feels right. It's still just as massive, just as special, just as full of possibility. Maybe I'll drop in on that skateboard ramp one more time . . .

Joel Little was born in Auckland in 1983. He attended Western Springs College and Mainz music school before forming pop punk band Goodnight Nurse in 2001. In 2009 he co-wrote the hit "My House" for Kids of 88 and moved into production. "Royals" which he co-wrote and produced for Lorde was number one on the US Billboard charts for nine consecutive weeks and won song of the year at the 2014 Grammy Awards. It appeared on the album Pure Heroine *which has been certified triple platinum (three million sales) in the US. He received a Golden Globe nomination for "Yellow Flicker Beat" from the* Hunger Games Mockingjay *soundtrack. He has since worked with local and international acts including Broods, Jarryd James, Ellie Goulding, Sam Smith, Tove Lo, Fitz and the Tantrums and others. He lives and works in Los Angeles with his New Zealand-born wife Gemma Robinson and their daughters, Lila and Emmie.*

Joel Little at the bat.

Deck, Westmere: Philip Patston's best view.

Philip Patston

Deck, Westmere

The oak tree is adorned afresh with foliage again. I've seen it go from bare to lush nearly 20 times now. Each year I shudder to think how empty the sky would look were it cut down — its deciduousness must play havoc with the gutters of the house beneath it. I wonder if I'll ever photograph the oak tree's annual cycle. I've been thinking of doing that for years. It'd make a great stop-motion montage, like the 10-day flowering period of the pōhutukawa at the bottom of my Westmere garden did last year. But I'm not disciplined enough to do anything for 365 days straight.

Unlike the oak, the pōhutukawa hasn't always been here. I planted it after burying Zarr there 15 years ago — my first dog, a German shepherd-doberman cross who couldn't help howling to music — and I'm always grateful that it reminds me of him. It hasn't flowered as well as it did last year, so I'm glad I didn't go to the trouble of photographing it. It wouldn't have been worth the effort.

The deck I'm sitting on, admiring the view that makes me forget I live just 10 minutes from Auckland's chaotic CBD, hasn't always been here either. The good old Kiwi deck. My deck. I sit here whenever I can, taking in the oak and the pōhutukawa, as well as others, including the mānuka, the puka and the quince tree. I sit amongst their branches, as if in a nest, sharing their beauty with the monotonous, territorial tūī, skittish sparrows and monarch butterflies making the most of their short lives.

I didn't build the deck, but I like to take credit for creating it. I called my Housing

New Zealand tenancy manager every month between 2000 and 2005 to ask him if it would be possible to have it built. Originally there were stairs at the back door, so in order get to the garden I had to go out the front door and around the house. I didn't have a powered wheelchair back then so it wasn't worth the effort.

After five years, perhaps I wore my tenancy manager down, or maybe he felt bad that I had only one egress, which I'd remind him was a fire hazard. Or maybe the stars aligned. But most likely it was just a matter of timing. HNZ implemented a maintenance programme in 2004 and my tenancy manager agreed to get my house put on the list. I had three meetings with an architect to discuss a major renovation — walls moved and removed, new carpet, a new kitchen and the deck, complete with a ramp. That wouldn't happen these days.

'In today's urban, cluttered, high-rise world, I feel lucky on a daily basis to have this place of serenity, safety and beauty, so close and accessible.'

Actually, the stars must have aligned because the renovation happened to start as soon as I left for a two-month work trip to New York and London. They didn't align quite well enough, though, because when I returned the job was still incomplete and the house looked like New York's Ground Zero. But that's another story.

Let me add more context. I have a neuromuscular dysfunction due to brain damage caused by a lack of oxygen at birth. As a result, I live with unique physical function and experience. That's how I prefer to describe my situation, but the common vernacular labels me disabled with cerebral palsy. Despite the prognosis that I'd be unable to talk, walk, learn or live independently, I've done all four quite competently — except walking, to be honest, which I gave up in my mid-40s. I'm well-educated, with an undergraduate diploma in applied social studies (social work). I've worked for the Human Rights Commission, run my own business since 1998 and had a reasonably successful career in stand-up comedy, for which I received a Billy T Award in 1999. I quit doing comedy after 15 years, in 2009, and I now provide professional consulting, speaking and project management services in the rather nebulous areas of diversity, complexity, change and leadership.

I travelled overseas regularly playing comedy and disability arts festivals; now I travel domestically about once a month for work. Travelling is effortful and tiring, which brings me back to the deck. As well as being a place to admire nature, over summer — and especially the holiday break — it becomes my retreat. Nature is known to produce endorphins and oxytocin — "feel good" hormones — so as much as I can at this time I relax, rejuvenate and reject the craziness of the festive season.

But it's not just me alone on the deck, though that is a common occurrence. The deck is a social place too, and often a hive of creativity and entertainment. Weather allowing, over the years, by day it has incubated many an idea and strategy, admittedly some not as successful as others. Covered by an electronic awning, it becomes a scenic boardroom, inspiring plans and initiatives from leadership programmes to music videos and children's books. By late afternoon, it morphs into an open-air bar, with strategy and planning turning to straw-sipped Merlot and playful banter. By nightfall, pizza arrives, and music and plenty of inebriated laughter echo from its warping, unoiled boards.

In today's urban, cluttered, high-rise world, I feel lucky on a daily basis to have this place of serenity, safety and beauty, so close and accessible. For, me the importance of the feeling of open space, particularly outdoors, is palpable. When I think back to other places I've lived, where I've looked out to fences and hedges, a sense of claustrophobia engulfs me. From the deck, I can see trees in neighbouring streets and even the spire of the Sky Tower through the branches of the oak tree. The landscape has changed over time: I used to have a view of Cox's Bay, but trees now obscure it. The right of way that runs alongside my property used to be visible and hence I was visible from the driveway. Now a burgeoning Bougainvillea offers privacy and another visual delight.

A few years ago I had two hostile neighbours over a 24-month period. It was a time of fear and anxiety for me. The deck lost its safety as my house is semi-detached, so next door is the same house. Once the second neighbour left, it took me several weeks to feel confident to sit on the deck again. For two years I'd lost not only my sanctuary but also, I realised, my gratitude. Life without either is empty. I remember the joy of their rediscovery and hold them dear now, more than ever, having been without them.

I'm writing this a couple of weeks after Christmas Day 2015, which was my 48th birthday. For pragmatic reasons my family celebrates Christmas together on Boxing Day or a few days after, so the 25th has become my day of celebration. As has become usual over time, from midday to midnight, a steady flow of family and friends, including a few overseas visitors, escaped the festive flurry to join me for a dram on the deck.

The washing line stands its ground amongst the flora and fauna, as does the rusty old shed at the bottom of the garden. In comparison they are eyesores, yet they add a rustic, imperfect element to my view. Similarly, the pots that hold the plants around me on the deck are in varying states of disrepair. The table and seats are looking a bit tired too. Someone remarked on the variety of styles of furniture the other day, making me rush online to research the cost of a whole new suite. It wasn't cheap.

Now I look back at the garden and notice the incredible paradox of nature: the unending cycle of growth and decay; the neatness and messiness; the light and shadow — all anew. Suddenly I am clear about the magic of the deck: it is a wilderness amongst the wilderness of my garden, which dwells in the wilderness of the world. My life is its own wilderness — rambling and constantly changing, growing and decaying, perfect and imperfect, alone and together.

Once again I notice gratitude and sanctuary. I'm calm and safe; everything is okay. And I wouldn't have it any other way.

Philip Patston has over 25 years' experience in counselling, social work, human rights promotion and leadership. He was a professional, award-winning comedian to boot. One of the Top 10 diversity consultants in the inaugural Global Diversity List, he is the recipient of Arts Access Aotearoa's inaugural Accolade for lifetime achievements promoting inclusion in the arts. Philip is an alumni of Leadership New Zealand, the New Zealand Social Entrepreneur Fellowship and Arts Regional Trust's Creative Entrepreneur Programme. He lives with his greyhound, Meg, blogging regularly at www.philippatston.com. He's author of a considerable collection of poetry, some of which he has put to music.

Philip Patston and friend on his deck.

Portland Road, Remuera: the Roberts residence.

Kevin Roberts

Portland Rd Remuera

I came to New Zealand in 1989 to join Douglas Myers and friends in their Lion Nathan adventure — an adventure which eventually led to buying Alan Bond's breweries in Australia, building a state-of-the-art Pepsi-Cola bottling plant in Sydney and a brand new brewery in China — and then to a sale to Kirin and a new adventure as Chief Executive Officer of Saatchi & Saatchi Worldwide.

We set up home in Auckland, and built our dream home in 1992 with architect Noel Lane in Portland Road, Remuera. The home is set in an acre of native bush, full of kauri, palms, tūī, cicadas and a meandering stream. Our three kids were brought up there, and now their kids are enjoying the thrill of the Fairy Garden, the Jungle Fort, Tilly's House, and all the non-health-and-safety approved tree climbs and rope swings the densely foliaged New Zealand outdoors can offer — at the bottom of their bedrooms and only 15 minutes from Parnell, Newmarket, Mission Bay and Saint Heliers.

Where in the world could you get that? Complete privacy, birds and insects galore, trails to explore, dreams to follow and The

> **'Over the years we've hosted endless games of hide and seek there, scavenger hunts, picnics, night-time fairy vigils, tennis matches, touch-rugby challenges, cricket tests, tree-climbs, and treks to Neverland, Treasure Island and Narnia.'**

French Café and Euro 15 minutes away (not to mention proximity to Eden Park, home of the Auckland Blues and stronghold of the All Blacks).

Over the years we've hosted endless games of hide and seek there, scavenger hunts, picnics, night-time fairy vigils, tennis matches, touch-rugby challenges, cricket tests, tree-climbs, and treks to Neverland, Treasure Island and Narnia. Only last week, four year old Cameron brought Superman and Batman to Tilly Plum's house for a Superhero breakfast. Six-year-old Kendall brought her Princesses.

And we've also shared the magic with corporate leaders too — as I hold retreats at the house for local and international leaders — and we use the bush for some sense-heightening changes of pace — where people can see how an environment can increase creativity and open up freer thinking.

In the fast-moving world we live in, a VUCA world — Volatile, Uncertain, Complex and Ambiguous — it's a joyful gift to have our own piece of New Zealand bush, smack in the heart of Remuera. Living well is the best revenge.

Kevin Roberts and family in a garden designed for fun.

Kevin Roberts has been Chairman of Saatchi & Saatchi — one of the world's leading creative organizations — and Head Coach of Publicis Groupe, the Paris-based global communications group. Kevin's latest book is 64 Shots: Leadership in a Crazy World. *Born and educated in Lancaster, Kevin started his career in the late 1960s with London fashion house Mary Quant. In 1989, Kevin moved to Auckland, to become Chief Operating Officer with Lion Nathan. From 1997 until 2014 he was CEO at Saatchi & Saatchi based in New York. In 2004, he wrote* Lovemarks: the Future Beyond Brands, *a ground-breaking business book published in 18 languages, showing how emotion can inspire businesses and brands to deliver sustainable value.* Lovemarks *was named one of the ten Ideas of the Decade by* Advertising Age *in 2009. In 2013, Kevin, a New Zealand citizen, was made a Companion of the New Zealand Order of Merit (CNZM).*

Waiatarua Park: a haven away from home.

Mai Chen

Waiatarua Park

When I lived in Wellington, my favourite landscapes to walk or run in were Tinakori Hill or Oriental Parade. Since moving to Auckland, I have discovered so many places I like to walk or run in, especially near water.

A favourite is Waiatarua, a beautiful wetland reserve near Mount Wellington which allows you to do a 3.2 kilometre loop while your dog is legally off-leash, barking at birds and sniffing and chasing other dogs and swimming in the ponds and rolling in the grass or worse! The challenge is keeping the dog out of the wetlands.

Our current dog overlapped with our golden Labrador, Socrates, for 10 weeks. Socrates was very old but she still loved to swim in anything bigger than a puddle, and she passed that love on to our new puppy, Pippin, before she died. But Pippin is a border collie and does not swim like Socs did. Rather, she soaks in ponds or streams like a hot tub or wallows in the water like a hippo. She stares at you as if to say, "That other dog taught me to get into the water, but I don't have any natural instincts as to what I should do once I am here."

So we have a border collie that displays Labrador characteristics — she loves getting a pat from strangers and eating the bread left for the ducks. But she also runs like the wind and I love to see her free and happy, meeting other, equally happy off-leash dogs of all shapes and sizes.

We get to witness the sometimes absurd combinations of dogs and owners. Big guys with poodles and pink track-suited women pushing prams with rottweilers and pit bulls with metal-studded collars.

I love the beauty and the variety of the Waiatarua landscape. I love the enormous green fields (perfect for throwing a Frisbee for Pippin, who is a champion catcher) and the wetland and especially the forest (bordering the wetland and the Remuera Golf Club) which is always full of birds singing. At dusk, when I often walk there after the day's work is done, the birdsong is deafening. No matter how many times I walk that track, clockwise or anticlockwise, there is always something new to see and enjoy.

> **'At dusk, when I often walk there after the day's work is done, the birdsong is deafening. No matter how many times I walk that track, clockwise or anticlockwise, there is always something new to see and enjoy.'**

It is my local, and my favourite place. I often run around it. Twice around is nearing 6.5 kilometres, and you don't have to worry about cars. You can just meditate, talk to your family about the day's happenings or listen to music while you walk or pound the track. I often solve complex legal problems after a walk, or find peace if my soul is troubled by the cares of the world.

This Christmas, we also discovered the Hūnua Ranges Regional Park and I spent a happy day with my family and dog tramping to the dam and back to the Hūnua Falls via a ring route. I loved the quiet meditative nature of the walkway through dense bush and towering overlapping tree ferns. My dog loved all the ways she could get wet in the numerous streams and waterways on the walk. The bellbirds were captivating. The cover of the trees cool and calming. We watched a movie that night about walking the Camino de Santiago. My husband and I had talked about walking it before, but after the meditative walk through the magic of the forest around Hūnua Falls, I really wanted to tackle the 800-kilometre pilgrimage during the school holidays, although our 12-year-old son didn't see the attraction of walking a minimum of 25 kilometres a day in summer heat carrying your own pack.

I almost always have my best ideas when I am out walking or running or swimming somewhere beautiful. In January 2015, the idea that came to dominate that year for me, to write about superdiversity, dropped into my head while I was doing sprint practice at Bloodworth Park. We were just back from three weeks visiting Argentina, Iguaçu Falls, Chile and Uruguay. One minute the idea wasn't there, the next it was and I knew this was what I should do. *The Superdiversity Stocktake: Implications for Business, Government and New Zealand* has now been downloaded more than 100,000 times since it was published in November 2015.

That is why I have loved reading Frédéric Gros's *A Philosophy of Walking*, which describes how great philosophers like Thoreau, Nietzsche and Rousseau worked while they walked in nature. I also read *Brain Rules* by John Medina, which explains that our brains were built for walking 19 kilometres a day, so it is no wonder that I think best when I am walking and running. If you want to improve your thinking skills, move. I wear my Apple watch which still records that I do a minimum of 10,000 steps every day and a lot more in the weekend. As a product of two elite athletes, I have always been happiest thinking and creating when I am moving. Mum and Dad tell me I am hyperactive. I tell them that it is their fault that I have so much fast twitch muscle.

When I think about why I love being a New Zealander, it includes my love of walking in beautiful places and being able to see clear skies and to be able to breathe clean air.

After immigrating to New Zealand when I was six, I spent most of my childhood outdoors. If I wasn't on the sports field before, during or after school, in the Dunedin town belt across the road from our house with my first dog, Zachariah, walking or running, I was fishing off the rocks with my dad. We had a crib in Hampden in the South Island, near good fishing holes. I jumped around the rocks and found bait and discovered things while my dad fished.

On a recent Christmas holiday, we cycled the new cycleway starting from Greymouth. It was gorgeous and varied, but it confirmed for me that walking in a beautiful landscape is superior to cycling for meditation, ideas and simple enjoyment. My bottom, back and knees don't hurt when I walk, and I don't need to concentrate on not skittering on the loose gravel roads nor changing gears to get up hills, or being careful on corners.

Some years ago, I did a somersault on my mountain bike trying to avoid a cat. I nearly severed my arm from my shoulder and landed in hospital. My AC joint would never be the same again and still hampers my back bends in yoga. As a result, I now cycle like a little old lady driving her first car.

If I couldn't be a lawyer, I would be a tramping guide. Bliss would be to get up every day, walk all day amongst great landscapes, and create new ideas.

Mai Chen is Managing Partner Chen Palmer, Chair of the Superdiversity Centre for Law, Policy and Business. She is also Adjunct Professor at University of Auckland School of Law, a Director on the BNZ Board and Chair of New Zealand Asian Leaders. Mai was also inaugural Chair of New Zealand Global Women. She was a top 10 finalist in the 2014 and 2016 New Zealander of the Year Awards. In 2016, she was named in the top 50 Diversity Figures in Public Life in the Global Diversity List affiliated with the Global Diversity Awards, which produces the annual European Diversity Awards, and is supported by The Economist. Mai was born in Taiwan, immigrated to New Zealand in 1970, and has celebrated her 30th wedding anniversary to Dr John Sinclair in 2016.

Mai Chen on the fitness trail.

Onehunga: the style of its public spaces
gives away the suburb's age.

Robert Sullivan

Onehunga

I grew up in Onehunga, near the old part with the blockhouse and the Fencible cottage, but I was always a city kid. My kindy was in Myers Park, which Mum would wheel me and my sister to along Grafton Bridge.

Before my parents bought a house in Onehunga, I remember the long drives we'd take with us kids in the back as my parents would look at suburb after suburb imagining where we'd all live once we moved out from our flat in Grafton with the bathtub up on planks near the hall ceiling to catch the leaks. Mum and Dad would talk about houses in the car. Some of them were way out west, on the way to Cornwallis with our pipi bucket in the boot — the house with the walls and roof made of the same wooden tiles not far past the dam which we'd talk about as it slowly went up over years— until we finally decided to move to Onehunga.

Like I said, we lived in Grafton first, until I was seven. I painted the footpath with my feet with the hippies on Boyle Crescent. They could've been in Baxter's *Jerusalem Sonnets*. I'll never know. Mum said Baxter was never any trouble. The Med School was still being built with its new concrete walls with the angles for running up and down — I remember being amazed at what an echo was, and the hieroglyphics on the doors that must have said "push" or "pull". I use that memory of seeing letters in a writing exercise: write a poem based on your earliest reading experience. The Domain, across the road, was our playground (there were trees to climb, and old elevators in the museum with cages). When we went to Onehunga it was the Jellicoe pools just up the road near the memorial arch, and a little later the public library.

A big part of Onehunga was the bookshelves of the Carnegie Library. During story time, a children's librarian would read to us. On my own, I would find books by Willard Price, or Enid Blyton, or books about the Roman Empire and the Russian Revolution, or books about science and travels to the moon or through the solar system, all from Onehunga. I had thousands of books just down the road, and could borrow five at a time.

As a Saint Peters wolf cub, the Anzac parade was a big deal. We'd march with the veterans up the Mall along Grey Street into Jellicoe Park past the memorial arch to the honour roll outside the pools. Wreaths would be laid. "The Last Post" would be played. People would line the street watching. I also remember falling down the concrete steps on my forehead outside the Saint Peters church hall during intermission for *Batman*, but my Aunty Hemo still finished the movie with my brother and sister while I moaned beside them. Pow.

It's funny fudging a love letter to a place that doesn't exist anymore.

Robert Sullivan at home in Onehunga.

Robert Sullivan is an award-winning poet whose nine books include the bestselling Star Waka *(Auckland University Press, 1999), which has been reprinted five times, and translated into German (Mana Verlag). As well as poetry, he has written a graphic novel, a children's book, a libretto, and co-edited three major anthologies of Polynesian and Māori poetry. He is Head of Creative Writing at Manukau Institute of Technology in Auckland. Robert belongs to the Māori tribes Ngāpuhi, and Kai Tahu, with affiliations to Ngāti Raukawa and Ngāi Tai. He is also of Irish descent.*

Hill Street Blues

I learnt to drive on a Falcon 500 without a handbrake
on Hill Street. It was the clutch that stopped her rolling back
from the crest of the hill as I'd dangle to turn left
giving way on Grey Street then turning wide
past Jellicoe Park onto the flat stretch to Newmarket
where Dad ran the pub. I'd pick him up after work—
about 10.30 each night after I'd got my licence
from the milk-man. Glad the petrol tank
Dad welded on with his mate didn't fall off
while I was driving. They cordoned off
a little bit of Khyber Pass with fire engines
for an afternoon. Then we got a new car,
a Cortina. Onehunga for me wasn't just
the Library. It was the roller skating rink
and making eye contact. It was badminton club
or soccer club and the time I saved a goal
against Mangere Bridge. It was the jogging
up One Tree Hill for the intermediate harriers,
and the recycled scouts hall on Grey Street.
It was the gifts we'd get from Mr and Mrs Coates
every Christmas, and the fruit and veggies
every other week from them. It was our old place
which is overgrown now, sold up.
We've all moved away, some of us
to other towns, and some to Oz.
But at least Karetu, Mum's village
in the Bay of Islands, is still there,
and that's the place to call home.

Still love Onehunga though!

Karaka Bay: where everything seems to turn to gold.

Joan Withers

Karaka Bay

We have lived in this location for 10 years, which is the longest I have stayed anywhere in my life.

Karaka sits on the eastern foreshore of the Manukau Harbour and is about 40 kilometres south of central Auckland.

In the early days of European settlement, before the Great South Road was forged, travel to the area was generally by water. The most direct route was across the Manukau Harbour from Weymouth to Karaka Point. The ferry service started in 1859 and according to local folklore, horses used to make the crossing swimming next to the ferry.

Our property was part of 8000 acres, much of it bounding the Whangapouri Creek which, subdivided into 70 farms, went up for sale by auction at the Chamber of Commerce building in Swanson Street Auckland in April 1914.

The Walters family home, which was built in 1920, was the main homestead in our immediate area. It has been lovingly refurbished over the years, and since we cut down a wind break of diseased Leyland cypress we have a wonderful perspective across the paddocks to the property. Looking in that direction one could be fooled that little has changed over the intervening years. The rural dimension of the area has always been attractive and even as the wider area develops and the population grows, the expanse of green fields, well-trimmed barberry hedges and estuary views are used by marketers to bring in people who are looking for suburban amenities on a country fringe.

It is a cliché but the sense of relaxation is palpable as the vista changes within a couple of minutes of leaving the Southern Motorway. The added benefit for us is the ability to keep and ride our horses on the property and enjoy the sense of community with other like-minded rural enthusiasts.

Karaka is famous for horses, not only the internationally renowned bloodstock sales complex but the enormous diversity of equestrian activities that take place in the area — thoroughbred studs, dressage, show jumping, eventing and for many many years until recently, the Pakuranga Hunt was based just a few properties up the road. The spectacle of the opening morning of the hunt was a reinforcement of the fact that rural life, even for a lifestyler, is very different.

> **We have many fruit trees which require a summer ritual of preparing bottles of plum sauce, late autumn preserving apples and figs and late winter making numerous varieties of marmalade. The preserves are very useful for taking to dinner parties and for encouraging tradespeople to respond positively and quickly the next time you call.**

There are adjustments and arrangements that we have to make to live on a property this size alongside horses, dogs, cows, sheep and chickens. My husband works full time but gets up early to feed the animals and tend to any urgent chores. We have some help with garden maintenance and with ensuring the horses are well cared for and ridden at least three times a week. If we go away we have a young couple who stay on the property during our absence. So it is certainly not a matter of lock up and leave.

We have many fruit trees which require a summer ritual of preparing bottles of plum sauce, late autumn preserving apples and figs and late winter making numerous varieties of marmalade. The preserves are very useful for taking to dinner parties and for encouraging tradespeople to respond positively and quickly the next time you call. A surprising number of my corporate colleagues are also into making preserves, so there is quite a lot of trading that goes on in CBD offices.

The compromises involved in living on the outer edge of New Zealand's biggest city, as opposed to right within its heart, have become fewer. There are now choices of cafes and restaurants, there is a first-class country market, offering at least as much as the inner-city gourmet markets, there is an outstanding private school and all the services and support needed for a lifestyler who spends a significant part of the week on other activities.

I cannot imagine moving into a smaller property. My recently acquired Fitbit tells me that on the weekends my step count is at least triple my weekday average. The animals provide a focal point and interest and being able to accommodate a pony for when our granddaughter and other young relatives visit and see their joy and developing skills as riders is a special pleasure. None of the work is a hardship, and over the years of our rural lifestyle we have had to make a pact that on the weekend or during holidays at no later than 3pm we relax, depending on the season, either by the pool or in front of the fire.

The contrast in the space and the outlook we have here compared to the numerous properties I grew up in as a child is perhaps the main reason why I am so attached to where we live. At this juncture, moving into an apartment complex, however well appointed, would feel too much like going back.

Joan Withers is Chair of Mighty River Power and Chair of TVNZ and is a director of ANZ New Zealand and The Treasury Advisory Board. She was formerly Chair of Auckland International Airport and has been a director of many of New Zealand's largest listed companies. She is also involved in The Tindall Foundation and the Louise Perkins Foundation (Sweet Louise). Joan left high school with School Certificate for a job as a bank teller. After spending time at home following the birth of her son, she forged a career as a media executive, eventually holding CEO roles in The Radio Network and Fairfax Media. In 2014 she was awarded the New Zealand Shareholders' Association Beacon Award. In 2015 Joan was named Supreme Winner of the Women of Influence Award and was Chairperson of the Year in the Deloitte Top 200 Awards. She is the author of A Girl's Guide to Business. *Her interests include horse riding and entertaining and she lives in Karaka with her husband, Brian.*

Joan Withers numbers horse riding among her passions.

Lynda Hallinan

Port Waikato

In the summer of 1989, the year I turned 14, the year puberty propelled me over the precipice from parental deference into defiance, I learned what it was to be free. To be self-sufficient, self-contained, to go off grid, my only worry in the world what species of fish we'd eat for dinner.

Frankly, my teenage self wasn't impressed.

I was raised on a small farm in the sticks: Latitude 37.350717, Longitude 174.901362, should you care for the GPS co-ordinates. In the summer of 1989, my parents decided to take us on a holiday from the backblocks to the boondocks, as if growing up in the Onewhero district — home then, as now, to roughly one per cent of Waikato's population — wasn't a cruel enough fate for two tempestuous teenage daughters.

In the summer of 1989, we set off for the West Coast via a gravel road less travelled. When we came to a one-way bridge over a creek in the crook of a dog-leg, Dad's mate Neal dropped us off and we tramped — some of us more gaily than others — along the Waikawau Stream all the way to the Tasman Sea.

We were freedom campers before it was controversial. We carried everything in, including a dunny spade, and carried everything out (or at least everything non-biodegradable). The packs on our backs contained, among other things,

Port Waikato: reputedly a difficult landscape to love.

four sleeping bags, three wetsuits, two pup tents, a box of Weet-Bix, milk powder, a bag of flour, a block of butter, a cask of red wine, melamine picnic plates, a frying pan, a sack of homegrown spuds and a Swiss army pocketknife for whittling driftwood into knives and forks.

On our first night, we pitched our tents on the side of a hill. It blew like a bastard, wrenching the tent pegs out of the sandy turf. One metal peg shredded my parents' fly sheet, another punctured Dad's unboxed wine bladder. My mother sympathised with my father as my sister and I delighted in the universe's black humour.

> **❛It was the scene of my worst sunburn; my lips so blistered they bled for a week. Sunset Beach, and rum and Coke, was to blame for my first hangover; my first New Year's Eve snog, with a local shearer; and my second, with an apprentice panel-beater from Taupō.❜**

You won't find the path we took in any New Zealand tramping guide. For five days and four nights, we followed the sheep-rutted tracks around the headlands on our way north, pitching our pup tents on the beach one night, in a gully by a freshwater spring on another. We feasted on pan-fried snapper if we were lucky, rock cod if we weren't, followed by Mum's griddle scones with a dollop of homemade Damson plum jam. One night we ate flounder; I'd speared the unfortunate flatfish with a barbeque fork, having stepped on it while swimming in the Huriwai stream.

It was undeniably bucolic, unless you were 14. I feigned indifference to the picture-postcard sunsets, the starlit skies, the phosphoric surf, the squid ink sands and refused to smile for the camera, sulking every step of the way to Sunset Beach, Port Waikato.

Te Pūaha-o-Waikato. Population: 1006.

Situated 88 kilometres south of Auckland, Port Waikato — The Port, for short — is where our nation's longest river greets the Tasman Sea. Quite a gob it has, too. On maps, the mouth of the Waikato River sports an obstinate Habsburg jaw. Waiuku sits upon its upper lip, its palate cleft by the mining of ironsand ore to fuel the Glenbrook steel mill, its epiglottis forested with *Pinus radiata*, while to the south the spit protrudes like a textbook example of mandibular prognathism.

It is a difficult landscape to love. Port Waikato lacks the grace and good looks of its big city sisters Piha, Karekare, Bethells and Muriwai, and the surfie chic of its hipster sibling to the south, Raglan. Its hillsides sport a crowning halo of gorse and scraggy sideburns of noxious pampas rather than native pōhutukawa.

It's a bit rough around the edges. Antony Starr never stood, shirtless and sombre, under a waterfall at Port Waikato and Holly Hunter, mute and melancholic, never played the piano here either. On the plus side, unlike at Piha, no one wasted a cent objecting to the establishment of a cracker of a local café in the old beach store at The Port, and just as well, too, because Sylvia's serves bloody good burgers, not to mention braised goat or tarakihi with kale pesto.

Aucklanders: pay attention! You can still bag a seaside shack here for half a million. Real-estate agents rarely fawn loquaciously over its falling-down fibrolite baches. They ain't retro. They're just like that, like they've always been, like they were when all the local sheep farmers in the district owned a bach at The Port.

As a child, it was the closest beach to my home. It was the scene of my worst sunburn; my lips so blistered they bled for a week. Sunset Beach, and rum and Coke, was to blame for my first hangover; my first New Year's Eve snog, with a local shearer; and my second, with an apprentice panelbeater from Taupō.

The Port was an easy 30-minute drive from our dairy farm. We could bundle into Dad's Cortina after the morning milking, spend all day blitzing quad bike trails across the dunes at Big Bay, inside the river mouth, and be back home in time to empty the udders in the evening.

"The very essence of romance is uncertainty," declares Algernon in Oscar Wilde's *The Importance of Being Earnest*. Port Waikato has plenty of that. Its physicality is imperfect, the landscape as amorphous as my ardour. Its stormy surf is all too often dirty, the spit disproportionately long (and a bit dull to walk the length of), the dunes too steep, the spinifex too sparse to anchor its shape-shifting sands.

For the past decade, Sunset Beach has been slowly and steadily undermining itself. Environmental reports commissioned by the Waikato Regional Council estimate the annual pace of erosion at two to five metres. This year it will be closer to five. The surf lifesaving club's patrol tower, which was forced to retreat inland in 2008, is again under threat. It now stands, nervously, less than 10 metres from the high-tide mark.

Half the carpark was claimed by erosion in 2012, the same year The Port's wild westerlies scoured out a skeleton buried deep in the dunes. It was Jayne Furlong, a mother, daughter, partner, police witness, prostitute. In 1993, when she vanished from Auckland's Karangahape Road, she was 17. As a journalist, I covered the police investigation into her disappearance, never once suspecting that her body lay beneath the same dunes we camped in as schoolchildren.

Does her murder tarnish my love for Port Waikato? Not particularly, for my affection was never Silvo-shiny. I love it the way a sports fan loves their team even when it's losing, like an old classmate I no longer have anything in common with, yet feel obligated to befriend on Facebook. I'm bonded to this place through history and convenience, loyalty and a little guilt.

I don't go there enough.

Lynda Hallinan is an author, columnist and broadcaster. She lives at Foggydale Farm in the Hūnua Ranges, south-east of Auckland, where she looks after an expansive organic garden and a mongrel menagerie of non-economic units including a blind Captain Cooker pig, two kunekunes, a clutch of free-range chooks, some feral sheep and a dozen fattened cattle. She also has a husband, Jason, and two children, Lucas and Lachlan, all of whom prefer Piha to Port Waikato.

Lynda Hallinan's enthusiasm for Port Waikato goes back a long way.

Louise Wright

Hahei

From my office window on the brow of College Hill I've landed a money-can't-buy view of Auckland's cityscape. To the south-east there's that tangled web, Spaghetti Junction, clogged with rush-hour middle management commuters swearing at another traffic jam that can't hear, then to the centre there's that geographically ubiquitous Sky Tower. And when this city dumps its daily rain bucket — as is its wont — that vista is, to be honest, all manner of concrete greyness; a little dull and flat yet kind of intriguing nonetheless.

But beyond this vantage point, when the fickle weather gives up so the sun can finally shine, far, far away into the distance I can see that spectacular place where my bliss begins. The Coromandel. It leads to the spot where over the hill and a little further away is Hahei. My heaven on earth.

Hahei and I met an age ago, a couple of years after my broken heart was finally ready to give the fingers to mourning, and the universe — along with my loyal friends — told me enough. It was time to get my mojo back. Despite perceptions, in reality I'm quite a self-contained, private person. And I had a five-year-old son to think of. So, when a few weeks after meeting Pete, I agreed to a weekend away at his family bach, it wasn't so much out of character, but more a considered move. We drove out of town in the old Toyota, popping in to see my brother first, although I can't remember if this was a gesture on John's behalf to protect his big sister, or me just wanting to say I think this kind and happy, oh-so-funny man might actually be something.

It was late on Friday night by the time we navigated the storm from Kōpū to

Whenuakite en route to Hahei. The story goes I fell asleep along the drive, but it's a lie. I did wake up. Just in time to see the wild pig and her piglets cross State Highway 25a from Sailors Grave Road. Within 10 minutes I stood on the deck overlooking Mercury Bay, and under that ink-blue sky saw my first satellite scoot across the horizon. There's only one streetlight that end of the Hahei valley, but I'll swear the place was lit up like Harrods at Christmas. Alpha and Beta Centauri may be four light years away, but with the Southern Cross and the rest of those celestial beauties that sky painted a canvas that I could only have dreamed of when hankering for the New Zealand landscape while living in the UK in the 1980s.

> **'But it's not just this exquisite landscape that's locked in my heart, it's because as a family Hahei bonds us. It's the fact that when we're here, we all seem to have time.'**

Most courtships run something like romantic dinners, bunches of flowers and French champagne. But not us. It was an early morning tractor ride on Te Waka Toa (everyone in Hahei has a tractor I soon discovered) at a 5kph pace along the squeaky white sand to Luna Cafe for coffee and free-range eggs fresh from the farm up the road. It may have been May but I swam that day — too happy and content to notice if it was cold. And I laughed and laughed as this city kid had a whirl at the wheel of the family Massey Ferguson. That night we drove to Ferry Landing where Pete whistled the Whitianga Ferry from the wharf on the Esplanade to cross the shallow river to take us to dinner. We sat at The Fireplace, long since closed down, and talked till they shut for the night.

Weeks turned to months and Hahei became our place, a sanctuary where, without the pressures of work and complications, we could slowly get to know each other and discover places and spots that to this day I feel blessed to have seen and experienced. We talked more in those days about what really mattered than I think I'd ever done in my then 40 years. I still thank Hahei for being that magic spot to make it happen. Because it was there, I at last told Pete, he had my heart. Fast forward, and my son is now 18 and living overseas but before he departed on adventures of his own, Pete and I made it official with our daughter, Millie, as flower girl, James giving me away and Pete's middle son, Tim, best man.

Geographically speaking Hahei has some pretty sharp credentials. A small settlement near Cathedral Cove, its beauty is second to none. I kind of think of it as the Angelina Jolie of Southern Hemisphere beaches. As a summer playground it's spectacular. Exploring the nearby caves by kayak, or snorkelling at the southern end below the pa at the Hahei Marine Reserve is one big mind explosion. I'll swear that the sugary sand that squeaks when you walk is almost pink, and the water is, at its best, like glass. Here the sea is so pure and transparent you can, beerpot willing, see your toes when waist deep. I reckon the 400 or so locals who have the pleasure of calling this place home must wake up each day feeling like they've won Lotto.

But it's not just this exquisite landscape that's locked in my heart, it's because as a family Hahei bonds us. It's the fact that when we're here, we all seem to have time. It's the coming together of the extended whanau where no one is in a rush that creates the ongoing magic. I always have a wee chuckle wondering how long it will take Uncle Gavin to get "that bloody boat" fixed and sea-fit, what menu Aunty Sally and I will create for the hordes to eat that night, or marvel how the holidaying kids grow taller each year, yet those childhood beach friendships endure despite limited contact in term time. As a baby, all chubby and bouncy, Millie had her first swim at nearby Flaxmill Bay. Her big brother James swam with dolphins when the mother and her pup followed us back with the jetski from Cathedral Cove one January afternoon. Millie fell asleep in my arms as we watched these amazing mammals swim with holiday-makers.

Wet winter walks are as exhilarating as any summer day. Just staring down the beach across to Mahurangi Island, making pronouncements about the height of spring tide waves, can wile away a good hour or two. Then it's time for a drink. Or three. On such days I delight in defending my Scrabble champion status. However our very vocal family tribunal over-ruled my creative word play last time. "What's an ig?" my son asked. "An Eskimo's house without a loo," I suggested. Overturned.

Hahei's not just the place, it's the memories and that overwhelming sense of happiness that we all get when you drive down that hill and turn right along Pā Road. I love the Hahei Store where I'm pretty sure if you asked if they had a set of blank BASF cassette tapes they'd say yes. They definitely have a good supply of candles and Beehive matches for the frequent power cuts in the valley. (You soon learn to take a bit of cash on holiday in case the latter does happen, as EFTPOS is a no-can-do in that situation.) The Florence Harsant Library is an institution. Fifteen dollars is all it costs for annual family membership, a tiny token I know, and the wonderful volunteers there will take a cheque too. (I had to explain to Millie the other day what a chequebook actually was. She was surprised. As was I that I still had one!) That's the special thing about this place, though, that old time-stands-still thing. Books, should they be returned outside the appointed library hours of 10 till noon, can be simply left in a plastic supermarket bag, the borrower's name inked on the outside. And don't worry if you inadvertently head home with your borrowed holiday reading. Just courier the books back — to the Hahei General Store. That shop with all manner of goods and produce will ensure the printed word gets returned to its rightful place. Now you don't get that with a Kindle.

There's a picture on my desk that I often, in my mind, jump back into. In this shot, printed for posterity, are my most precious people and it represents all that I love and cherish. There they are photographed against the Hahei cliff face beneath a flowering pōhutukawa. James, aged eight, with his overly-long Hallenstein's board shorts and holding his new Nike soccer ball, bought as a holiday treat. His best mate, Jack, stands by his side; just as he was the morning we farewelled James to England this summer. Then on the picnic blanket sits my darling Pete, in a wetsuit that once fit (but perhaps may have shrunk since then) holding Millie our love child, who at six months old is all chubby and toothless with the happiest face and a life ahead full of hope and promise. It makes me smile every time. This is the place I want to be. And the place, when my time on this Earth is done, I'd like to stay. As I said, it's heaven.

As a redhead born in the middle of an Otago winter, Louise Wright had the odds against loving summer stacked against her. But the beach and the North Island's Coromandel Peninsula are her happy place; for the warmth and the sea. And hanging out with her family. When not working for her not-for-profit charity, aka kids James and Millie, she's been employed as a journalist for 25 years from daily newspapers to stints as editor of New Zealand Woman's Day — twice — *and* New Zealand Woman's Weekly. *She is currently executive director at PR agency Porter Novelli.*

Louise Wright and daughter Milly at the beach.

Theresa Gattung

Waihi Beach

I was born in Wellington but brought up in Rotorua, so going to the beach was always a novel experience. If we went to the beach from there we went to Matata, but that's a fishing beach, not a swimming beach.

There are lots of wonderful things about Wellington, but one of the joys of Auckland that I discovered when living there was that so many wonderful beaches were so accessible.

However, when I went to Waikato University to do a business degree, I met John, my now ex-partner, and his parents had a house at Waihī Beach.

We started going there all the time. I fell in love with the place and we bought a bach there. When we separated much later, I kept that place and now have built a house next door to it for my parents. They've retired there. It's become the family enclave where my sisters come and stay too.

Both houses are cedar. Mine's double storey and currently looking like it needs a repaint. Theirs is single storey, because as you get older there are mobility issues.

Thanks to the two houses, and having my parents based there now, Waihī means family. It means winding down and relaxing.

I love it partly because, having

grown up in the Bay of Plenty, it is quintessential Bay of Plenty. Waihī Beach sits at the intersection of the Waikato, Coromandel and Bay of Plenty. It's got that irresistible combination of bush and beach and that laid-back feeling.

There aren't a lot of big, ritzy holiday homes at Waihī. It's not Ōmaha or Papamoa, and it's not trying to be. It's got a great, relaxed vibe and the shopping centre is cute as. It's got wonderful cafes. It's got Allpress coffee. It's got everything you need, but you don't have to put on make-up to leave the house.

I'm surprised it's taken people so long to discover these areas, especially given what a million dollars can buy you there compared to what you'd get in Auckland.

I even love everything about the drive there, from the moment I turn off the motorway and head towards Ngātea, then winding through Paeroa and into the Karangahake Gorge, which is amazing. Before you know it, you're at Waihī, which has had a bit of a renaissance with the gold mining. And when you come over the brow of that hill and see the beach laid out — it's a great feeling.

It hasn't had a lot of pressure from developers. There are still plenty of places you can camp or rent for a week or two.

Yes, there's building going on, and there's always people selling and buying. But the beach has many entry points and people hang out at the surf club. There are no gated communities.

> **'I even love everything about the drive there, from the moment I turn off the motorway and head towards Ngātea, then winding through Paeroa and into the Karangahake Gorge, which is amazing.'**

It's still about the great natural beauty and the amount of space with no crowding. It feels like there are more people here than there were when I started coming 30 years ago, but there are more people everywhere in New Zealand. Our population has gone up, and that's a good thing.

It seems to me that at Waihī, at least, the desire for development and actual development have kept pace nicely. Some people have got the builders in and made their places a bit bigger. And some are still in cottages that they've had in the family for generations.

I get there as much as I can, which is not always as often as I would like. During the year I'll get down for an occasional weekend. In summer I go for between two and four weeks. Friends come and stay for a day or a weekend or a week.

It's a pleasure being able to share this with other people. My house is set up for that. It's beachy. There's no carpet. I want people to be able to walk inside with sand on their feet and not worry about it. You've got to be able to relax when you're relaxing.

And it's all about doing simple things — swimming or walking on the beach and collecting shells; pottering in the garden; hanging out with the family.

I have no trouble switching my work brain off there.

Because it's so central we often make day trips to Hamilton, Tauranga or Rotorua. But above all it's a classic Kiwi family experience.

Perhaps because my business focus is now on My Food Bag, I'm not a holiday cook. I like baking but

I don't tend to do that at the beach. I don't save up recipes to try. In fact, I've never been much of a cook, which may be why I thought My Food Bag would do so well.

Above all I feel very settled when I get here. When we bought this place, John's father had spotted it. If you live somewhere you know the good areas. So we bought the old house and lived in it as a beach house because when we built we wanted to get it right. We wanted it to be built in the right position for the sun and so on. And we did get it right.

Theresa Gattung is a leading New Zealand business personality and author of best-selling autobiography Bird on a Wire. *From October 1999 to June 2007, Theresa was the CEO and Managing Director of Telecom New Zealand, where she led the company through world-changing technology developments. Over the past few years Theresa has been involved in a wide spread of governance positions in both New Zealand and Australia. She also co-founded the hugely successful start-up, My Food Bag, which has a turnover of around $100m. In 2015 she was made a Companion of the New Zealand Order of Merit for services to business and philanthropy and also inducted into the TVNZ New Zealand Marketing Hall of Fame. Theresa is involved with a number of not for-profit and philanthropic interests, including being co founder and trustee of the Eva Doucas Charitable Trust and the World Women Charitable Trust, patron of the Cambodia Charitable Trust and chair of the Wellington Board of the SPCA.*

Theresa Gattung proving how easy it is to relax at Waihī.

Grande Vue Lodge: horses were an important part of life on the property.

Vaughan Smith

Grande Vue Lodge

Grande Vue Lodge was my grandparents' farm, a name I think they gave it because there were trying to posh it up. And, maybe because of the name, I thought it was a very lovely farm. I always loved it. It had a forestry block with a waterfall at the back, and there was a creek with river rocks in it like you see in picture books.

It's in a part of Matamata called the Peria Hills that backs onto Hobbiton. From the back of the farm you can see the Hobbiton border. And on a clear day you can see Ruapehu.

It wasn't really a lodge where people stayed, but it fit the criteria of a lodge in one respect, because they had horses, and if you have horses you're either a stud or a lodge.

Actually, they had a bit of everything. There was dry stock in the form of sheep and beef. And there was a big chicken shed with chickens that weren't exactly free-range, but they could walk around a bit. It was definitely the smelliest and noisiest place I knew when I was a kid.

My brother, sister and I went there all the time, because the members of our family lived very close to each other. When my parents went out with friends, instead of getting a babysitter, they sent us to my grandparents' place, which was only a 15- to 20-minute drive away.

Because Mum and Dad were both home-based and worked on the farm, having three kids constantly pestering them for something to do in the school holidays was too much so they unloaded us onto the grandparents for at least a week each.

My brother would go first. Then I'd go

halfway through the first week. Then I'd have some time by myself. Then my sister would come and I'd share some time with her. Then I'd go and she'd have some time with them to herself.

I just assumed that's what everybody did when they went to their grandparents'.

At Grande Vue we were given tasks. And when we left, we got $5 and Nana took us into Matamata and bought us a book and hired a video. We thought we were onto a good thing, but we had been working for hours scrubbing thistle and painting fences.

At home with Mum and Dad, we weren't made to get up early to help with the milking, though, which is a bit weird because now I do breakfast radio I have to get up at the same time as dairy farmers anyway — though I don't have to put up with being out in the cold.

> **'At home with Mum and Dad, we weren't made to get up early to help with the milking, though, which is a bit weird because now I do breakfast radio I have to get up at the same time as dairy farmers anyway.'**

But at Grande Vue, as well as doing jobs, we also got to do stuff our parents wouldn't. They had a mower that we were allowed to ride like a motorbike if we mowed the lawn properly.

I have a vivid memory of Gangey, our name for our grandfather, with us in the ute — he pulled the choke out, put it in second gear and climbed out the back to throw out the hay while we were inside steering. We would have been three, five and six and we were fighting over who would steer. That was pretty loose.

Our paternal grandparents also had a farm nearby. They had sheep and beef as well, but their farm didn't have a name. They were Nana and Poppa. Nana loved being a grandparent but Poppa didn't know what to do with kids.

My grandmothers were two very different people. Dad's mum was like a textbook 1950s New Zealand housewife. She had bone-handled cutlery and she baked non-stop and you got fed non-stop.

Over at Grande Vue, Mum's mum used to bake too, but more often she was out on the bike herding sheep. When I met my friends' grandparents, they seemed really old, but mine never did because they were always doing things. It used to blow my friends' minds when I told them my grandmother could drive a motorbike. When my granddad bought the property, it wasn't a horse farm. It wasn't anything at all really — apparently it was a total mess. But when he started talking about having horses, someone told him he wouldn't be able to manage it so he thought, "I'll show you," and he did.

There's a stubborn Irish-Scottish streak in the family which means we will always do anything people tell us we can't.

He had breeding mares and used to look after other people's as well.

I didn't really get into the horse side of things. I had an aunty, who married into the family, who did dressage and that sort of thing, and my sister had a pony that reared up and stomped on her head.

But I learnt a lot about horses and other aspects of life, because they were breeding thoroughbreds. According to what I was told, to qualify as a thoroughbred, a horse couldn't be the result of artificial insemination but had to be conceived naturally.

I sometimes had to help and it was always the same old story. The mare would be in the holding bay and there was a little horse called the teaser that would nip the mare to get her in the mood. Apparently that's reassuring for her.

Then she would release a pheromone that a stallion could smell from 200 metres away.

Someone had to collect the stallion, who would be going crazy, and lead him to the mare. They had to put slippers on her rear hooves in case she kicked the stallion in the wrong place and rendered a million-dollar horse infertile.

And it was someone's job to wash the horse's penis and guide it so that a million dollars did not end up on the ground.

On one such occasion, when I was about eight or nine years old and everyone was going crazy — people and horses — Granddad yelled at me: "Wash that horse's dick and put it in the mare."

He poured me my first shandy that night.

Some years later, when he was 70, he was taking a horse back to the paddock after breeding. They're not sure if the horse bolted at the gate or at him, but when they found him he'd fallen off his bike and had brain damage. He had a couple of seizures and spent the last few years of his life in a high-care facility.

My nan and my uncle and his wife still live at Grande Vue Lodge. After Granddad's accident they sold off the front half of the property, and they live on the back part, which is arguably the more beautiful part. It's still running but it's a smaller operation.

We live in the city, so my two daughters haven't had the chance to grow up with the farm as part of their everyday life. But they love going there just as much as I did.

Vaughan Smith, born and raised in the Waikato, now resides in Auckland with his wife, two daughters, a dog (an 'oodle of sorts) and a $48, 11-year-old rescue cat. Although a West Auckland urbanite, his heart still pumps rural blood, which is like ordinary blood except a bit grassier, and spends a lot of time with his kids at his parents' Waikato dairy farm. He also lives dairy farmer hours, as he wakes at 4.20am to take part in his weekday morning ZM Breakfast show. He's worked for Fletch in the radio game since 2004 and has also dabbled in the odd TV project, some involving panel shows, has written an article or two for print, eats on camera for an internet series called Critic and the Pig, *and often does colouring-in competitions under the name of his children to win prizes.*

Vaughan on the farm with his grandfather, Ted Smith.

From the shores of Lake Rotorua, Mokoia Island is an irresistible lure.

Scotty Morrison

Kawaha Point

All of Dad's father's generation owned land around here. Then our koro moved into Ōhinemutu village, so the others sold up and moved into the village as well, but Dad ended up staying out at Kawaha Point. That's why we are there, while the rest of the family is in the village where there is a whole block of Morrisons living next door to each other, papa kāinga style!

Dad and his brothers built our house. He and Mum moved into it before I was born and I was brought up there. My sister is back there, as well as her son and my brother.

I'm the youngest of four with two brothers and a sister. I wasn't planned according to Dad and he would always jokingly let me know: "You're just a mistake, boy, but I was in fantastic form the night you were conceived!" When Dad passed away he lay at home for a night or two before he went down to the marae.

Our homestead at Kawaha is the sanctuary, where people in the family go if anything is going down or if we want some time out. If I ever need to be somewhere where I can regenerate physically, mentally or spiritually, that's where I go.

Mind you, it helps that Mum still spoils me when I go there and does all my washing and cooks all my meals.

That is the way Mum is. It's an open-door place. All kinds of people turn up and get welcomed there. If our movie star cousin Temuera walks in he'll get treated the same as one of my sister Andrea's hippie mates, like royalty.

Mum's garden is immaculate. It's always on the programme when there are tours around the house. She's in her seventies now but she's always out there — sometimes from dawn to dusk — doing the garden all by herself. She still walks to work at Rainbow & Fairy Springs where she's been for nearly 40 years. And she takes a rubbish bag with her and picks up rubbish on the way to work.

We have a strong ancestral connection to the location. There is a lot of history tying us to it.

About 30 metres to the east there is a cave where our grandfather was brought up for the first few years of his life. Another ancestor, Tunohopu and his family were being pursued one time and, needing refuge, hid in that cave.

> **It was awesome because it was so safe. We could ride our bikes round and round without having to worry about traffic. And there was some bush in the middle with big trees where we could play war games and hide and seek.**

It's still there but you have to know where to look, because it's hidden under willows and can only be reached by boat.

When we were kids we used to go and play there. Back then you didn't worry about life jackets. We got in the boat and paddled off down there to play in the cave with our action men figures.

There are other aspects of history to acknowledge. For instance, the name of our section is Mokonuiarangi. It's named after one of the paramount chiefs from the Green Lake area who they reckon was responsible for the killing of the nephew of Hongi Hika, which led to Hongi coming down and ransacking Mokoia, the island in the middle of Lake Rotorua where Tūtānekai wooed Hinemoa.

They went there thinking he would have come on foot and wouldn't be able to get across the lake to where they were. But he was ingenious and split his canoes into three pieces so he could drag them overland then join them back together and launch them on the lake.

Mokonuiarangi fled during the battle and swam to the shore and safety with everyone chasing him. The ones who stayed behind on the island got slaughtered by Hongi's people but he escaped. The spot where he came up out of the water is where our house is, which is why the property is named after him.

So when I am at home and looking around, I can see history in every direction.

With all this tradition there is an expectation that the property will stay in the family now, so it's a responsibility for the next generation.

And it is still my home sweet home. I still regard it as the place where I reside spiritually, even if physically I live in Auckland. And Stacey's and my three children were born there — we went back for their births and that has added another layer to the history that is rooted in that spot.

It was important to us that they were born somewhere where their bones were, even though Stacey is from the South Island. Their whenua are buried in Rotorua, with trees planted over them: a tōtara, a kōwhai and a karaka. We took their cords to the South Island and they are buried there.

The land around is all residential now, but when we were growing up there were very few houses. The section next to us was vacant. The site is basically two cul de sacs making a looping road, so it's a dead end. It was awesome because it was so safe. We could ride our bikes round and round without having to worry about traffic. And there was some bush in the middle with big trees where we could play war games and hide and seek.

On the lake side we took our little polystyrene surfboards, grabbed our lunch and paddled down to the stream to play all day and come back at night. And no one ever worried about where we were.

One day, when we were about 12, my Pākehā neighbour mate and I thought we'd emulate Hinemoa and swim out to Mokoia. His father said he would follow us in his kayak, so if we got tired we could hold on. But we did it. We used to go there quite a lot and swim in Hinemoa's hot pool.

Now you have to get permission from the trustees to land on Mokoia but we still swim in the lake, and my kids jump off the diving rock outside our house, like we used to . . . and just like us, they'll spend all day playing on the beach in front of our house.

You see history repeating. The neighbours have been there as long as us. We grew up with all their kids, and now we see their kids running around with ours.

Scotty Morrison (Ngāti Whakaue) is the well-known presenter of Māori current affairs programmes Te Karere *and* Marae Investigates. *He holds a Diploma of Teaching, Bachelor of Education and Master's degree (Education) from Waikato University, and is currently working towards his PhD at AUT University. Scotty has been an Adjunct Professor and the Director of Māori Student and Community Engagement at Auckland's Unitec Institute of Technology, where he continues to promote te reo Māori through awareness, administration and specialised courses. He is also the author of the bestselling* The Raupō Phrasebook of Modern Māori *and* Māori Made Easy. *Born and raised in Rotorua, he now lives in Auckland with his wife Stacey Morrison and their children, Hawaiki, Kurawaka and Maiana.*

Scotty Morrison as a young man, with friend.

Napier Hill: the location used to be an island and is still a centre of marine activity.

Nick Malmholt

Napier Hill

Mataruahou — a name I never knew. Until now. Shame on me. Because I love Mataruahou. Always have, always will, and always called it simply the Hill. Because that's what it is. Big, beautiful and the only geological megalump in town. My town. Napier.

Where all is flat. Except for the Hill. It used to be an island; with ocean and lagoon lapping all sides, but not quite an island by the time Cook's *Endeavour* loomed into view. By then Mataruahou linked to the mainland with tenuous spits of sand and shingle, caressed by creeping swamps.

Perhaps the Hill will be an island again, if perfidious climate change has its drowning way. It better get a wriggle on though, because climate's not the only awesome nature game in town. The sea might be rising fast, but around the Hill the land is rising faster still.

It rose with a bang and a lurch in 1931. Big earthquake. Goodbye, lagoon. And goodbye to any claim the Hill once had to be an island. And goodbye to Great Granddad Olaf's chimney. His daughter, my Mormor, Rona told me all about that frightening day when the earth shook, buildings fell, fires raged, and people died.

And she told me all about it on the Hill, in Mormor's little wooden house on Shakespeare Road. Kids in Napier discover the road on the Hill long before any inkling of the long-dead, famous guy it was named after. And on that road my three-year-old self stubbed his three-year-old toe walking up the Hill with Mormor after buying my first ever dinosaur book. Milestone on Mataruahou!

From dinosaurs to debauchery. My 15-year-old self staggered to another milestone, in another little wooden house, on the very same Hill. I got drunk for the very first time. Blind drunk. Literally. That flagon of cheap sherry guzzled on the Hill stole my eyesight for a night, and gave me nothing but fun times and vomit in return.

> 'Because the Hill is where shit happens. The sexy and seedy, the come hither dreamy, the forbidden and hidden, it's all on the Hill. The twisting, turning, leafy, labyrinthine Hill, with old houses, old money, and original sin, stands in stark contrast to city and suburbs sprawling flat and flabby below.'

But return I did. Back to the Hill where school kids inveigled our under-aged way in to swill beer to the music of Kiwi band du jour the Dance Exponents. To be fair, the notorious pub selling booze to boys and girls (back in the day) is barely on the Hill. Topographically it's just a mere few metres up the first gradual slopes, but culturally, emotionally, obviously, it's very much on and of the Hill.

Because the Hill is where shit happens. The sexy and seedy, the come hither dreamy, the forbidden and hidden, it's all on the Hill. The twisting, turning, leafy, labyrinthine Hill, with old houses, old money, and original sin, stands in stark contrast to city and suburbs sprawling flat and flabby below.

Perhaps that's a bit harsh. But as a flabby, flat, Hawke's Bay suburbanite of long lounging, I know of what I bleat. The one Hill to rule us all is our collective touchstone, with myriad messages and meanings. It's our lost idyll, our shameful past, our colonial splendour, our usurped utopia, our squalid decay and our gentrifying, speculating, painting-and-decorating future.

As well as many meanings, the Hill has many names. Ignored and forgotten by Pākehā, if ever known at all, Mataruahou is the moniker bequeathed by Ahuriri Māori and only recently, grudgingly accepted by the Crown. Long before this belated Waitangi wake-up, the British christened the Hill Scinde Island. Named, apparently, after Sindh Province in India. How very Empire. How very Raj. Much like Napier itself.

Scinde Island never caught on. But Napier Hill did. Not exactly poetic, but pragmatic and clear. Shortened soon to just the Hill — it's the only hill we've got so why waste time and syllables? But sometimes you need to get specific, and to many the Hill is more multiplicity than monolith. The east end is Bluff Hill. The west end is Hospital Hill. Though perhaps not for long. The hospital is freshly demolished, so it's a healing hill no more.

Before the hospital, in times more military, the west end was Barrack Hill. Maybe now, in times more mortgaged, it can be called Overpriced Apartment Hill. Bubbly and predictable, that's what's going up. Why have a hospital? Get granite bench tops instead.

I shouldn't sneer. As the centuries tick by, real-estate chancers have been working their haphazard magic on Mataruahou. A barren lump, long denuded of bush, the Hill now flaunts botanic beauty, terraformed with Monkey Puzzle exotica and spiky native delights. It's a vision of hope and a garden of promise, hinting that us so-called sapiens aren't all bad all the time. We truly can make things better, greener and sweeter, even if only accidentally.

Imagine the good we could do if we set our hearts to it. The Hill stands tall and verdant in Napier, urging us to reap what good we might sow. Our homes cluster in a hill-sized beehive, nestled in flowers and trees, as we burn our finite candles and die. Great Granddad Olaf died on the Hill. And Mormor died there too. Sunrise, sunset, our Hill is always there.

Our solitary Hill. Napier's rocky outcrop of human promise and progress. We helped make the Hill a better place, and the Hill inspires me to try and make my short life and giant world a better place too. So much to do, dreams to pursue, if I only had time — on the Hill.

Nick Malmholt travels the world but will always call Napier home. Unless another giant earthquake flattens it, in which case all bets are off. These days Nick mostly divides his time between Britain and New Zealand, with a whole lot of Skype and email thrown in. He earns a crust writing for the screens that rule our lives. It used to be called television, but the media platforms are all starting to blur these days — much like Nick's vision.

Nick Malmholt and his hill.

Taranaki: the mountain and a monument to past endeavour.

Paul Hartigan

The 'Naki

Under a stained red sky the State Theatre neon shone out like a rescue beacon, the thick air salty from the foreshore nearby. It was a classic Art Deco cinema, like any other found in similar towns around the country perhaps, but it was ours and therefore special. The impressive foyer, with the plush pile carpet in cacophonous autumnal colours (this was so luxurious; we had humble felt on our floors at home) the jazzy chrome fittings, huge door handles and sculptured lights, all so magically atmospheric. I'd seen *The Wizard of Oz* there in the late 1950s and Hayley Mills' *The Parent Trap* in 1962. At half time, older kids in white uniforms brought ice creams into the theatre, a big box tray with holes where the cones sat snugly before they were picked out for eating. They still played "God Save the Queen" before each and every film then too.

After the movies, in my brother's era, (he was eight years older than me) nothing was open except Ping's Pie Cart down by the train station — they stayed open until the morning's small hours dealing with the drunken Teddy Boys, Widgies and the like. I'd been there when I was old enough to be out late to see Daisy, the owner's beautiful daughter, a legendary waitress able to carry multiple plates on one arm and more still, on the other. An unusually tall, leggy China doll, her enormous beehive hair-do, a foot high, made her taller again, having an almost formidable effect, a truly gorgeous creature that my brother and his mates fantasised about for decades to come — that legend was fact, phew. In mild contrast to this old-school diner, we had new to town, right on main street The Arizona, selling

American style burgers and chips over a white Formica counter rather than sit-down meals — Californian contemporary cool, and they also had a fiery red neon sign burning in the black of late night.

Directly across the street was the fashionable La Scala Restaurant. They served à la carte, strong gin cocktails, Pimm's for the ladies, please, and played Frank Sinatra or Dean Martin relentlessly — sometimes Mario Lanza. Upon entry you traversed a bridge and Wishing Well water-feature complete with plastic ivy to enter into the expansive uber-contemporary Italian-styled dining room — this was New Zealand's award-winning premiere restaurant of the day, it was legend! Mum had work there, part time and I went once or twice for special occasions with the extended Lebanese family, usually a wedding, engagement or someone's 21st. It felt very adult and I was an inexperienced kid amongst so much sophistication. The Swing Bling place of the era, I still have their swish glossy menu from the day featuring prawn cocktail entrées, chicken cacciatore and carpetbag steaks — bombe Alaska for desert.

This was New Plymouth in 1969. Devon Street, our main drag, was eight kilometres long, and it followed the coastline to the city limits either side of the town centre. This abrupt eroding edge into the sea below is where our renowned "hot" sand, black with silvery iron, mixed socially with a myriad of dead cars and old fridges — no recycling in those days, just convenient dumping. The Taranaki shoreline was a place to explore, sometimes dangerous because waves could come out of nowhere and thump hard on the huge boulders sitting there, stacked up on top of one another like perfect dinosaur doughnuts. These benign behemoths were a beloved and persistent subject for local painter Michael Smither — how many of these giants has he painted in his lifetime? Our river stones were similar but usually of smaller size, I'd always wondered how these great rocks had got to be so perfect and round, like a nice arse. How does nature do that?

> **'That was really something, standing on the highest point possible to take view of half the country, Ruapehu, Tongariro and Ngāuruhoe all together, the curve to the south of the Wanganui coastline. Summer and shorts all the way to the top but the crater was filled with snow, still, brrrr.'**

Further down Main Street in the centre hub, the land dropped down topographically with an almost secret stream running beneath the town — the Huatoki River. You'd hear the sound of splashing running water and occasionally the river would come into view, draining into the sea nearby. The meeting of these different water types fascinated me. We'd had it overflow several times during that decade and around 1966 we'd had a tremendous flood that wrecked half the town, submerged the place badly and put a real damper on things for quite a while. You could see the mucky, dirty flood marks up the sides of shop walls for weeks afterwards. We in town were all comfortably situated on the alluvial flat land, ostensibly a beautiful setting amongst the solid green, but behind us loomed the mighty mountain — Mount Egmont as it was known then — and she shed water either through precipitation or massive run-off from melting snow. Generally it was just a natural blessing. I'd climbed to the summit with my school class, a couple of teachers and two guides in 1968. That was really something, standing on the highest point possible to take view of half the

country, Ruapehu, Tongariro and Ngāuruhoe all together, the curve to the south of the Wanganui coastline. Summer and shorts all the way to the top but the crater was filled with snow, still, brrrr.

In New Plymouth's central city downtown there were a number of key attractions for me, Tingey's Paint Shop being a favourite one. They had all the latest decorating fads on show and I was a regular visitor. In the display window there was always an array of oil paintings of the mountain for sale with price tags attached. Mum and I used to stare at them on a Friday night when the street was bustling — it always did on Friday. Various artists showed their work in this impromptu gallery space but the most competent, prolific and clearly skilled painter was Bernard Aris, an Englishman who'd come to Taranaki in about 1912. Aris was a painter of harbour ships in England à la Turner, but it was said that he'd fallen deeply in love with our magnificent Mount Egmont, then spent practically the whole of the rest of his life painting en plein air around the town and in the nearby regions of Inglewood and Kaponga. I'd had the luck and privilege to meet him then through my close friend Kari Scanlan, whose journalist parents had adopted Bernard to save him from starving to death through over-enthusiastic commitment to his subject, his snowy muse. He looked rather rumpled I remember, forlorn, of similar colouring and disposition to Van Gogh. I have some of his drawings and his field fob watch inscribed with his name, which I treasure.

Don Driver worked in that same shop behind the counter. He wore a clean, rather drab grey lab coat, was moderately tall, of almost silent disposition, his immaculate but masculine large hands had flawless nails. His hair, ever so slightly silver even then, was perfectly placed — not a strand astray anywhere on that noble head. He wasn't like most men of that time, not at all. He wasn't gay, he was just tidy — his art was just like that too. I'd heard a comment that he hadn't been allowed to wear long trousers until his twenties! Don's demeanour was always the same, always reliably lovely, a gentle man with a gentle spirit and a soft warm smile. As a much younger boy, I'd go in there and buy small cans of Dulux enamel paint to take home and paint my wooden swords with, or silver wooden spears embellished with the blood of my enemies — Don found this amusing and would offer useful "making" suggestions. Later I'd be buying enamel to paint household furniture or the kitchen walls. We were state house tenants and my mother, a proud housekeeper, sought to support where she could, the five or 10-year decorating government upgrades herself, with our help. Don and I shared a lot of conversation over the years and became avid art colleagues, even to where we exchanged ideas on the vitality of both contemporary art and hot local women alike. Although a married man, Don, a bit of a smooth Don Juan himself, was discreetly obsessed with the female species. This was around the time of *The Graduate* being played just down the street at the Mayfair Theatre, the arrival of Anne Bancroft into my life via the movie screen was a crash course in adulthood that up until that point, had not been fully comprehended. Go, Dustin.

I was now a fifth-form student at New Plymouth Boys' High, a school with a big reputation for being traditionally British. There were the unfortunate boarders banished from home, and the less despondent day boys. Fortunately I was one of the latter, altogether 1200 of us roaming the grounds. An almost equal number of girls were across the valley via a wide river at New Plymouth Girls' High, far enough removed for any potential liaison to be difficult at best. I didn't enjoy the old disciplinary regimes perpetuated by brutal masters — one such nicknamed "Fish", a bad asthmatic, was predisposed to beating you for the most incidental misdemeanour, along with the regular and insistent infliction of barbaric mud sports or high-speed balls, likely to remove young vulnerable teeth. Mine stuck out and were likely to go west; I'd been tormented over those many a time. No, a pencil, paper or paintbrush was my preference, ideally while listening to Cream's *Disraeli Gears* or Jeff Beck's *Truth*. My hair had grown longer in sympathy with the times and courtesy of the chemist shop turned dark auburn red — more derision ensued — "Bloodnut!" they shouted. Looking back, I'm really not sure what possessed me to dye my hair, but it would have been to mimic some mod from Merseyside, or perhaps Ray Davies — I loved The Kinks, so did my sister, Georgette.

Consequently I'd spent a fair bit of my time bunking school, I was either shore side searching the numerous rock pools for marine life in a self-educating exercise down by Kaweroa Baths, the public swimming facility, or in the obscure depths of Pukekura Park, the generous public recreational gardens and grounds that existed geographically between where I lived in Brooklands and my high school, near the Racecourse on Coronation Ave. From home we could hear the booming blare of the commentator and almost see the snort and sweat of pounding thoroughbred horses around the big oval track. The packed grandstands were huge, as were the enormous pine trees behind them, our textbook perfect mountain practically always in view of any local activity. I could see it perfectly well if I climbed onto our garden shed, the solid concrete bunker arrangement in the backyard which served as a pretend studio, tool and woodshed alike. I practised signing my name there on the wall with chalk. Soon after I'd discovered modernist maestro Picasso, watching him paint a huge white bull onto glass on our new TV. I figured I could be that too.

It was now the late-start beginning of the social revolution in New Zealand, hippies, trippies and alternative thinking suddenly sprang up like mushrooms in a Taranaki paddock — seemingly out of nowhere. People were perplexed; some mildly anxious, while others were in deep dread or even angry. Television was a burgeoning social medium and the reporting of Muhammad Ali, atrocities, disasters and the moon landing able to be conveyed in real time. We were enjoying watching *I Love Lucy*, *The Beverly Hillbillies*, *Bonanza*, *The Fugitive*, a tipsy Deano Martino and late at night *Rawhide* and *The Invaders*, a corny but somewhat unsettling program about weird invading aliens. Secretly I was worrying about potentially being drafted into the Vietnam War, God forbid.

So it was back to thinking, wondering and standing on the monster boulders again, looking out to sea with the sun in my eyes, to see if I could see Australia.

Paul Hartigan is an Auckland-based artist, whose career spans five decades. A painter, photographer and sculptor, he is best known for his large public neon installations in Auckland, New Plymouth, Wellington and Christchurch. He is the subject of Don Abbott's monograph Vivid: The Paul Hartigan Story, *published in 2015 and named best non-fiction book (Australia/New Zealand) in the 2016 Independent Publisher Awards. In 2017 he will install CINEMA, a new neon commission at New Plymouth's Govett-Brewster Art Gallery / Len Lye Centre.*

Paul Hartigan at home on the peninsula.

Hāwera: the water tower is never less than dominant.

Aroha Awarau

Hāwera

It doesn't lean like the one in Pisa or light up a Parisian sky, but the Hāwera water tower is unforgettable and sentimental to people like myself, who grew up in the South Taranaki township.

To be honest, it's a bloody ugly thing which is only aesthetically pleasing at night, when the red beams on its top shine over the street lights, giving the illusion to visitors who drive into the town in the darkness that Hāwera is much bigger than it seems.

The 55-metre tower was built in 1914, after fires in 1884, 1888 and 1912 destroyed several businesses, resulting in insurance companies demanding the water tower be built to provide the town with better fire-fighting capacity. Ironically, Hāwera means the burnt place, a name given to it after a local Māori tribe surprised its rivals by burning their village to the ground.

So Hāwera and its water tower represents fire, and fire is a symbol of passion. And passion is something that I, and others who leave Hāwera to chase their dreams, can relate to. I've always wanted to chase the bright lights, and I don't mean the ones that shone on top of the tower.

Many famous New Zealanders who hail from the town have

shown passion. Its sons and daughters have carried its torch and conquered the world. There's All Black Conrad Smith and former national rugby coach John Mitchell. There's netballer and former Silver Fern captain Adine Wilson. Hāwera's even produced three comedians: Ben Hurley, Alan Brough and Vaughan King.

We have an international reality TV star in Sean Kelly, who was raised on a farm outside Hāwera and won the thirteenth season of US fashion designing competition *Project Runway*. Kelly has swapped the Hāwera water tower for the Empire State Building, and now lives in New York.

But Hāwera's most famous son is novelist Ronald Hugh Morrieson, with whom I have a personal connection, being a writer myself and having been a three-time winner of a local literary award named in his honour.

> ❛So Hāwera and its water tower represents fire, and fire is a symbol of passion. And passion is something that I, and others who leave Hāwera to chase their dreams, can relate to.❜

I vividly remember Morrieson's family homestead from my childhood. It was on the main road and hadn't been cared for since his family sold it after Morrieson's death in 1971. In fact, it was really shabby and a child's dream. The house, which had been built by Morrieson's grandfather, looked like it was haunted. I remember it being used for community events that my family would attend. At the time, I didn't realise that it was the home to one of the country's most beloved writers. I played in the attic, where Morrieson penned his four classic novels, *Came a Hot Friday*, *Pallet on the Floor*, *Scarecrow* and *Predicament*, which all have been made into feature films. It's common knowledge that the locals loathed Morrieson due to his drunken antics, his womanising, and the fact he wrote about the underbelly of the town and not "nice stuff" like the parks and the quiet streets. The citizens would eventually get their revenge when they demolished his home to make way for a KFC. In 1992, fans tried to retain Morrieson's legacy and fought unsuccessfully to save his home.

He never left Hāwera to pursue his writing. He existed in obscurity in the town, and never lived to see his work become the success that it is today. His heavy drinking contributed to his early death on Boxing Day 1972 at the age of 50, and his novels become popular after his demise. He famously told mate and fellow novelist Maurice Shadbolt, months before he died, that "I hope I'm not another one of these poor buggers who get discovered when they're dead".

For a young writer like myself, those words from Morrieson were enough to inspire me to make the most of my opportunities, and that meant leaving the town after finishing high school to pursue a writing career. I certainly didn't want to become a poor bugger who was discovered after I'd carked it.

From the attic where he wrote, Morrieson would have been able to see the street and the imposing presence of the water tower. I wondered if he was inspired by it. I'm sure Morrieson would have climbed the water tower many times. I remember my first time as a five-year-old, and counting every single step, like an annoying child would do. There were 215 of them and the treat was the view that greeted me when I reached the top. As well as the town itself there was a view of another imposing figure that looms over Hāwera — Mount Taranaki. The residents of Hāwera have the unusual phenomenon of having not only an impressive manmade structure towering over them, but also a natural wonder. The mountain has a gothic feel about it — romantic in the summer and cold and harsh in the winter. No wonder there were dark and sinister events that occurred in Hāwera inspiring all of Morrieson's novels — the murders, the affairs, the sex, the mayhem. Who would have thought that this quiet settlement would represent the underbelly of the bleak, small, New Zealand town. It makes me wonder if the Hāwera water tower could talk, what other secrets it would share.

Aroha Awarau is Māori/Niuean and has enjoyed success in three different writing disciplines —scriptwriting, playwriting and journalism. As a former News Editor for Woman's Day *and Senior Writer for the* New Zealand Woman's Weekly, *Aroha won best magazine journalist for mass market titles two times at the annual Magazine Publishing Awards. His debut short film* Home, *premiered in Toronto, and in 2015 he won best short film script at the Māori Writer's Awards. He has written two successful plays. His first theatre work, called* Luncheon, *had a sell-out season in Auckland and won the award for best play at the 2014 New Zealand Scriptwriting Awards.*

Aroha Awarau with his mother Nina at Hoani Papita, a local Māori Catholic community.

Craggy Range: unkempt hair and a pocked visage.

Debbie Harwood

Craggy Range

On one side the beautiful Māori Chief Rongokako's form flanks the Heretaunga Plains. The sleeping giant — his coffee-coloured, silky magnificence prostrate and languishing for all to see. No wonder Hinerakau fell in love with you. How glorious you are.

But on the other side . . . the other brother.

The other brother . . . the one who will never comply . . . the one who never seeks adoration or lauding but longs for understanding and expression. The untamable rogue with the charming heart steeped in melancholy.

Dearest Craggy Range,
You are the one I love.
Craggy Range . . . your gnarly fists push up out of the silky hills, fighting for release from your rocky insensate form, longing to commune with the sky.
Requited . . . the light along your ridge intensifies as it brushes your ragged skin then flares into golds as the sun retreats.
Unrequited . . . I long for you to watch me . . . but your mute gaze is trained on places I will never see and deep in your eyes are knowings that no ancient scripture, scrawled by the wisest of our forebears, will ever be able to explain. And perhaps because of this my love will be strong for

eternity. I could look at you for a million years and still feel my inner world sigh every time my eyes soar to your craggy peaks. I want to run my fingers through your unkempt hair and stroke your jagged and pocked visage but no hand or war or force majeure will ever tame you or change you – we will all be gone and you will remain. If you knew me there would be a beginning to our love and then inevitably an end . . . so I will stay meekly in your shadowy gullies with my love for you its own reward.

Ragged rock 'n' roll range . . . while musicians fall like petals to the ground you will endure millions of mortal lifetimes . . . still breathtakingly handsome . . . with your wild, yet quiescent, swagger. What will I do when I can see you no more? I know! When my flesh falls and I am but spirit I will reside in you. I will dance along your ridges and tumble down your slopes. I will be your angel – that is what I will be . . . your guardian angel . . . as you have watched over me my whole, mortal life.

Our beautiful sun will scorch your precipices for as long as she burns. Please say goodnight to her for me when it is all over.

Love Debbie

Debbie Harwood in the place where her spirit will reside.

Debbie Harwood, after touring with her original bands and releasing three solo singles, formed When the Cat's Away, who were named Top Group at the New Zealand Music Awards — as well as celebrating a gold album and the No 1 single "Melting Pot". Since 1996 Harwood has produced several albums most of which were recorded at her recording studio in Devonport, "The Bus". When the Cat's Away toured and recorded again in 2001 and 2002 achieving platinum sales for their live album with Sharon O'Neill. In 2009 Debbie put together a stellar line-up of some of New Zealand's greatest women singer/songwriters. Called Give It a Girl, the show features Sharon O'Neill, Shona Laing, Margaret Urlich, Annie Crummer and Debbie herself.

TE MATA STORE
P.H.WATKINS.GENERAL STOREKEEPER

DENTIST

WATKINS STORE
TE MATA. N.Z. 139

G.BROS.PROTD.1.7.10.

The Rangataua Pet floats above the mountain.

Jenny Pattrick

Ruapehu from Rangataua

The mountain dominates us here: that great majestic — if rather ungainly — heap of volcanic rock that rises surprisingly out of the plateau. No great spiky backbone dotted with peaks like the Southern Alps. Ruapehu stands here alone. We pull the curtain in the morning and there he is. Or more frequently, not. Conversation is dominated by remarks like, "No mountain today," "Will he show himself later I wonder?" "Haven't seen him for a week." From our angle the other two volcanoes, Ngāuruhoe and Tongariro, are hidden. On a clear day the sun rises behind the mountain. We see a dark silhouette against pale sky; three rocky peaks thrust up from long muscular shoulders. Then the glaciers take shape, their snow catching the sun. We sit out on the deck over breakfast, watching as colour invades the view; the rocks and fissures, the fingers of snow if this is summer; the regal white expanses of winter.

In the foreground are the trees we've planted over the years, considering carefully whether they will grow too high and hide the mountain. Flaxes — the giant ones that grow up here — are best. Their prodigious flower-stalks attract bellbirds and tūī and they never

> **'We sit out on the deck over breakfast, watching as colour invades the view; the rocks and fissures, the fingers of snow if this is summer; the regal white expanses of winter.'**

need trimming. Larger trees — beech, tōtara, poplar, kahikatea — are planted to the sides of the section, framing the view. What is it about this long reach, from our backyard across the grass and flax and trees and up to the mountain that is so satisfying, so in tune, somehow? Perhaps that we have had a hand in shaping it over the years. Basically it is the presence of the mountain. No wonder Māori in the early days averted their eyes as they passed, recognising its power.

There is a phenomenon here known as the Rangataua Pet. I have no idea where the word "Pet" came from. It's a highly distinctive, mushroom-shaped cloud, its dome completely smooth and often the underside ominously dark. It sits a little south of the mountain in a sky that is usually clear apart from the Pet. The saying is that if you see a Rangataua Pet there will be rain within 24 hours. Usually an accurate forecast.

We started coming to Rangataua in 1970. Back then most of the houses were empty and owned by the Ministry of Works. The settlement was once a bustling milling town which grew up alongside the railway. It died slowly as the trees were cut. We put in a tender for the big old abandoned postmaster's house and won it for $800. The water tanks were rusted, the bathroom deep in mud, someone had had a porridge fight in the kitchen and the wiring was shot. But its bones were solid and it came up beautifully. Now four generations of the family have lived and holidayed here. Perhaps not long before a fifth generation looks out in the morning to see if the mountain is clear, or sits with a drink in the evening watching as the sun turns the snow deep pink, then a softer glow and finally steely grey. As the light fades, fat wood pigeons come in to land first on the rowan tree, testing the ripeness of the berries, then setting the kowhai trees thrashing as if a storm has arrived; those tender leaves are their delicious dessert. Then the stars. The night sky, up here on the plateau, is a marvel. Rangataua has few street lights (none when we arrived); the Milky Way arches across the sky, so bright, so intense that it could be alive. Perhaps it is. In the early days we had a long-drop at the

Jenny Pattrick on a break.

back of the section. On a frosty night the icy walk to the loo was made magic by that sky. Gerard Manley Hopkins' words were often quoted: "Look at the stars! look, look up at the skies!/ O look at all the fire-folk sitting in the air!"

Our children learned to ski on the mountain in the days when there were no lifts or tows — you walked up, you skied down. Their children have learned in a more genteel (and expensive) way. And all generations have walked, time and time again, the wonderful tracks that cross and circle the mountain, never tiring of the bush, the glimpses of the mountain and the great vistas back to the plateau. What a treasure this National Park is — Tongariro, the first to be created, the gift of Te HeuHeu and the Tūwharetoa people. Ngā mihi Tūwharetoa; thank you Department of Conservation and Ngāti Rangi for watching over it now.

Jenny Pattrick is a writer and former jeweller whose eight published novels, including The Denniston Rose, *its sequel* Heart of Coal, *the Whanganui novel,* Landings, *and* Inheritance, *set in Samoa, have all been New Zealand number one bestsellers. She has chaired the boards of many arts organisations including the Arts Council of New Zealand. In 2009 she received the New Zealand Post Mansfield Fellowship. In 2011 she and her husband, musician Laughton Pattrick, published the children's book and CD of songs,* The Very Important Godwit. *Her latest novel,* Heartland *was released in 2014.*

Donald Kerr

Ohingaiti

Ohingaiti is about 164 kilometres from Taumarunui, which was our starting point. Mum and Dad would bundle us — Stewart, Heather and me — in the car, a shiny black one, and head south. Egg and cheese sandwiches and Thermos tea were the order of the day. Our trek was a slow meander on the road through National Park, Ōhakune and Taihape. The Rangītikei River dominating. The wonderful white bluffs and tall trees; McIntyre country. When we hit Mangaweka we knew we were almost there. And then the infamous bend in the road, by the hotel. The flag would be flying. My grandfather, a farmer, a general overseer for the Rangītikei region, and a Boer War veteran, would always have the Union Jack flying on the flag-post by the gate. I don't know how long he and my grandmother ("Mom") stood there waiting for us to arrive, but they were always there. It was always a glorious reception for the Kerrs of Taumarunui. This was however the general rule: the Stents' house at Ohingaiti was open-home to all: third cousins, tired travellers, old swags. All were welcome; everyone got a warm reception.

The farm was large and encompassed many fenced acres of paddock. Wooden stiles were strategically placed for access to endless fields. My grandfather farmed both sheep and cattle. Many times I remember him hand-docking the lambs, with blood spurting everywhere. The dogs — Tip, Jock and Mac — flying about like whirling dervishes. And I remember well the stories my mother told me of her getting up at 4.30 am to hand-milk the cows. All of them had names: Bessy, Buttercup, Flossy. Indeed, their bellowing in the early morning was a comforting sound to a small child growing up, lying in bed and wondering what time it was. The whistle and toot of the train as it rumbled up and down the main-trunk line had the same effect. There was a constancy in Paradise. The farm was a regular menagerie, home to one-eyed magpies, donkeys, cats, and pet horses. One famed resident was Bibi the monkey, who was brought to the farm by my uncle, who was in the navy during the war. When Bibi escaped she caused havoc in the community. This donkey-riding, plum-eating glutton was eventually sold to a travelling circus.

On arrival, the first course of action was to run into the large kitchen, which not only exuded warmth, but always contained the smell of good food bubbling on the large coal range. This would inevitably lead to the spring sofa by the large window overlooking the garden. The sofa, covered by a multi-coloured crocheted rug, was a sacrosanct spot. It was where "Mom" played patience — endlessly. By watching her I learnt the rules.

The second course of action was to discover the outside, which although we knew well was always a new world. Outside we would revisit the sheds with the old onion bags hanging from the rafters, spot the tired and rusty horseshoes lying about, note the dog kennels and the dirt and grime from the farmyard, and be confronted by gates everywhere. One decree issued by my grandfather in his gruff voice was: "Shut the gates." Woe betide anyone who left a gate open. Skinned alive was his threat!

> **'The whistle and toot of the train as it rumbled up and down the main-trunk line had the same effect. There was a constancy in Paradise. The farm was a regular menagerie, home to one-eyed magpies, donkeys, cats, and pet horses.'**

The days spent at the farm oozed family — connections, gossip, laughter and cries — but I cannot remember what my dad or mum did during our stay, nor Stewart, my older brother by three years. I don't ever remember putting our bags down or going into the bedrooms, although I am sure we did at some stage. One vivid memory was watching my grandfather sit on a low stool in front of the coal range. He would slowly wind bandages up one leg and then another. Each bandage end was delicately pinned at the top. It was a methodical process and often he would seem dissatisfied with progress. Halfway through he would unwind, straighten, readjust and tighten the bandage, and then continue the winding. I was transfixed. Behind him on the wall were relics of his time in Africa: assegai clubs and cow-hide shields. He never talked about it.

One part of the farm sloped to a small stream. It was there that Heather, my twin sister, and I would have enormous fun. Old discarded water cylinders lay about, many of them punctured by bullet holes (my grandfather was a good shot). We would angle these large corrugated cylinders towards the stream and then proceed to get inside them. By running inside them they started to move. And of course there was no real control. Many times the cylinder would run askew, leaving us wondering where we were going. It was a free-wheeling time, rolling and tumbling over until we hit water — or something, like a stock water pump. Often we spilled out to see the cylinder roll towards the water by itself. Peals of laughter and "Let's do it again" would ring out. We would slowly wheel the cylinder back to the top of the slope, position it so we could get in and then repeat the leg movements. This was repeated endlessly until we were beat. There was always one downside: facing the wrath of Mum after she discovered the tears in our trouser backsides, caused by the jagged holes in the cylinders.

Another memorable occasion was the celebration of my grandparents' golden wedding anniversary — the big 50! This was true family-time: great aunts, uncles, aunts, and cousins gathered together and as the weather was fine, we amassed outside on the lawn. Chairs for the old folks; grass for the kiddies. A piper, speeches (my father taking the lead), toasts, and raised full glasses: "Pip, Pip!" The largest cake ever (at least to my eyes) was cut. One delight was sitting on my grandfather's lap, where he would angle the saucer to my mouth and fill me with warm black tea. Being stabbed by his bristly moustache was a danger.

I was raised correctly of course, knowing my manners. Heather went first. My aunt Aggie, who spent time as a missionary in India and China, looked on disapprovingly. She won my heart much later when I received as a bequest her own colonial edition of Emerson's *Essays*; I treasure this book still.

I don't ever remember the drive home to Taumarunui, but no doubt it was faster (as it always is) than the trip down. One solid fact remained: I always looked forward to a return to Paradise.

Donald Kerr is Special Collections Librarian at the University of Otago. Prior to his move to Dunedin, he worked in the Sir George Grey Collection at Auckland City Libraries. Before that, secondary school teaching and working in the publishing field. All a long way from Taumarunui and Rangitīkei country. He is currently working on a book about twelve prominent book collectors in New Zealand.

Donald Kerr waits his turn with the saucer.

A move to Palmerston North signalled the end of the years at Waiata.

Karl Maughan
Waiata to Palmy

Dad was known as Bill Maughan or sometimes C.W. Maughan, but I like Bill Maughan. He was a sort of strange character who wanted to be an artist and a writer. He worked in Treasury for a while in Wellington but was always wanting to get out.

Then he had a motorbike accident and got an ACC payout, so left Treasury and we went for a trip around the South Island — my parents and two kids from Dad's earlier marriage who needed a break.

When we came back from the trip, the Manawatu beckoned.

Dad had been doing a lot of writing with Geoff Murphy and Bruno Lawrence, and Mum had acted in their first film. Dad knew them from jazz club. They were involved in Blerta then, but that operation was such a family thing there wasn't room for Dad. He needed to do his own thing. That was a big part of leaving. It was quite good for Bill to leave Wellington and find somewhere new.

He wanted space and time to write his satire of life in the civil service.

He also wanted to get involved in landscape gardening with his friend Dave, who lived around there.

We looked around and found a place that didn't exist, called Waiata, near a town that did exist, called Plimmerton.

It was an old 300-acre farm at a time when such farms were uneconomical. There were empty buildings to be had on small lots, and we paid something ridiculous like a dollar a week to live on this farm in the middle of nowhere.

Suddenly, at the age of about eight, I went from being a town kid to a kid with long hair going to school on a country bus.

My parents were treated with unbelievable suspicion by the locals, especially when Dad painted a flower on our letter box. But that changed when there was a Scout bottle drive and they got three trailer loads of bottles from my parents' place and made more money out of them than everyone else put together.

I remember telling a kid at country school, "My dad's an artist." One of the older kids leant over and said, "Your dad's a piss artist." Which was funny, because he was.

So I roamed the farm for a couple of years and had a love affair with the whole area. A favourite part was where we could walk to a huge river valley where we could collect fossils.

> **'So I roamed the farm for a couple of years and had a love affair with the whole area. A favourite part was where we could walk to a huge river valley where we could collect fossils.'**

People would visit us, but we really were in the middle of nowhere.

I did make friends at school. I went to a school reunion recently, and the girl who was the looker and Miss Golden Shears in 1981 was there. I managed to find a full school uniform and wear it. No one could believe I had my socks down.

I thought the small school would have been closed down by now but a lot of people had moved into Feilding and Palmerston North wanting their kids to have an agricultural school experience, so now it's three times as big as it used to be.

Much later I did a project there with Chris Knox. He asked me if I had any ideas and I thought of painting the staff room, which was always grim. I built a little box and painted it to show what we could do. The principal was excited, but the school had grown so much and the staffroom was much bigger than I remembered. So I got the kids to paint too. I did big drawings of rhododendrons then cut them into squares and the kids had to paint them.

When I was there as a pupil, we had a headmaster who decided he would employ teachers based not on how they dressed but on their qualifications. He didn't care if they had long hair or bare feet. As a result, he attracted amazing teachers from across the country, including my wife's father, who is now a professor of maths in Auckland, and an English teacher who had us reading Voltaire.

But Dad decided the standard of education at the country school was slipping. So I got given a project he devised involving fungi. I had to slice them in half and draw them. I still have a big folder of those drawings.

At the time, I just thought "more mushrooms", but in retrospect it was a fantastic exercise. Even the experts find mushrooms that are unknown to them when they go out looking.

There were weird excursions out and around the Manawatu in the early days there. Dad and I started collecting old children's books, like the Little Golden Books, wherever we could find them. Then we started buying them in second-hand shops. It was a great adventure, travelling around finding these books and trying to outdo his friend who also collected them.

A lot of the kids books I collected are from towns that don't exist anymore. They were school prizes from the 1890s when books were very expensive. People would have kept these school prizes their whole lives, then their kids would have chucked them out when they died.

We were only there for a couple of years before moving to Palmerston North. Mum became a lecturer in agricultural economics.

Dad resisted actually buying a house for a long time, but eventually we bought one in Ashhurst (in Palmerston North). I was reading Fleur Adcock's autobiography and learnt that her family house in PN was somewhere we had rented.

For high school I had to bus from Ashhurst. I made lifelong friends there and some have ended up back in Palmerston North, where they have done a lot for the place. A couple set up a sculpture trust and a gallery so there's sculpture all around Palmy. Another runs a great online magazine called *Swamp Thing*. Another pair run a tee shirt shop called Pork Chop Hill, after the hill teenagers used to drive up to go snogging on Friday nights.

It's a difficult place, Palmerston North — it's in a permanent state of terminal decline that never quite happens. But because my friends are there I feel very connected. We get to hang out together and see each other. I slide straight back in.

Karl Maughan was born in 1964 in Wellington. He moved with his family to the Manawatu in 1973, and after attending seven primary and intermediate schools, (including Aokautere School for one day). He managed to stay at Freyberg High for all of his secondary schooling. He attended Elam in Auckland from 1983 to 1987 and had his first solo exhibition also in 1987. For 11 years he lived in London and has been painting, running cafes, delivering bread and wearing shorts for the last 29 years. He is married to novelist Emily Perkins and has three children. He lives and works in Wellington.

Karl Maughan waits for the school bus.

Pāuatahanui inlet's boat sheds and boats.

Kerry Fox

The road out of Stokes Valley

My place is a journey. I drive it a lot when I'm in New Zealand because I have a friend who lives in Paekākāriki who I visit, and my family come from the Hutt Valley. I come back to New Zealand once a year, so I make that trip a lot.

It's the one place I always think about and it's meaningful to me because getting to Haywards Hill on the way out of the Hutt meant we were leaving for our holidays. And coming back to where we lived, in Stokes Valley, you came over the hill and saw the valley ahead of you and that was the last leg before home which meant it was the end of the holiday.

The landscape is also partly a mental one because it's a combination of the area itself and the idea that roads in the north are really dangerous — and this one in particular. There were so many warning signs. I always associate travelling and holidays in New Zealand with road deaths.

It amazes everyone I know that I got my driver's licence the day I turned 15, but I did. In my family, however, you were ready to drive at 15 because our holidays always involved one of the kids being taught how to drive. We weren't allowed to get our licence until we could change a tyre and tow and reverse a caravan and a trailer.

More recently, as an adult, I've ridden my bike along part of this route because that stretch of road contains a lot of what New Zealand means to me. There's a Lighthouse Cinema there now and a very cool café, which always makes me think of how long it took for New Zealand to get decent coffee.

It's part of always being in the process of leaving or coming back — both when I was a child and when I travel that road today.

And there's a stretch of water that State

'We weren't allowed to get our licence until we could change a tyre and tow and reverse a caravan and a trailer.'

Highway 1 goes over — it's Porirua Harbour, really — which is always still because it has a tiny mouth and the entrance is protected.

When I cycle it now with my brother, from the groovy cinema to Plimmerton to the rocks, it's all changed. It's been super-duper updated with a cycle way along the edge of the harbour.

It's important as a connection that's been maintained my whole life, no matter what else I've done or where I've been. Sometimes I try to take my dad, or I will persuade other people to come on bike rides and make them stop at my important places.

When I was a child we usually went on holiday that way, although sometimes we would go over the Rimutakas and Martinborough way. Even then, however, the leaving or returning were the significant parts of the trip.

As was the car sickness. I got terribly, horrifically carsick. I once threw up a whole packet of wine gums down the side of the Kingswood.

Another memory that is triggered when I make the journey now is how different holidays used to be.

We had one holiday a year, when my father got time off at Christmas. That was really significant. It feels more so now when I think about the luxury I have of being able to choose to take a long weekend or go to all sorts of different places if I want to, especially living in Europe. I can take the kids away on their half-term breaks if I feel like it.

That was absolutely not available to us when we were little.

I come from a long line of flower growers. My mother's father grew flowers and my father's father grew flowers. My father grew flowers too but he worked as an accountant for a kitchen importing firm. And that meant one holiday at Christmas.

We made that journey to Taupō every year. My father would spend three days decompressing and then we would head off to another North Island beach for the rest of the holiday and camp there. That was the holiday. Same thing, every year.

But I didn't think of alternatives. I didn't know any different.

And now I also take my kids camping every summer here in the UK for a week or 10 days. We certainly don't go to the beach. We'll go somewhere where there is a beach, but you can't make that your destination because there will be only one or two days you could spend on the beach. It's freezing.

Also, in the UK, beach campsites are barren because of the wind and the cold. The environment just doesn't suit. You want to go inland a little bit. There are always fields that you can camp on and sit around eating and enjoying, not having to do anything. When you live in the centre of London, getting away from the city is an end in itself.

Kerry Fox is one of New Zealand's most internationally respected and awarded actors. Her body of work includes Jane Campion's An Angel at My Table *for which she was awarded the New Zealand Film Award for Best Actress, the San Sebastian Film Festival Award for Best Actress and the Venice Film Festival Elvira Notari Award for Best Performance; Gillian Armstrong's* The Last Days of Chez Nous *which earned her the Asia-Pacific Film Festival Award for Best Supporting Actress; and Patrice Chereau's* Intimacy, *which saw her win the Silver Bear Best Actress Award at the Berlin Film Festival. Kerry has appeared in numerous productions for the BBC, ITV and Channel 4 in the UK. In 2010, she starred in Rowan Joffe's BAFTA Award winning telemovie* The Shooting Of Thomas Hurndall. *She has recently starred in a number of Australian features including:* The Dressmaker, Holding The Man *and* Downriver.

Kerry Fox and brother on the road.

Chris Bourke

Lower Hutt

In 1998, my sister's play *Stash* was produced at Bats in Wellington. Every night the lead character, an elderly woman based on our mother, would utter a line that would make the whole audience roar with laughter. Until they recovered, their reaction disrupted the action.

The character is recently widowed, and the victim of a con; she is being driven around in a Holden Kingswood and the perpetrator is at the wheel. She doesn't know that, though. She is wearing Dirty Dog sunglasses and she is stoned. She doesn't know that, either.

"Everything has gone wrong since Dad died," she says, with a sigh. "We should never have left the Hutt."

It only took us 90 years. When it happened, my sister and I were in the same car, following the removal truck. Inside it were our mother's household possessions, minus a rubbish skip full of things that get stuck in the back of drawers. Funeral cards, broken spectacles, safety pins. As the truck joined the motorway into Wellington, with us in hot pursuit, my sister acknowledged the significant moment: we had finally left the Hutt.

Dad had died in 1995, and after a respectable amount of time — 16 months — Mum sold the house they had built in central Lower Hutt 37 years earlier and moved to Thorndon, another place of happy memories. As a young adult she boarded there in the early 1940s, after migrating to the city off a farm. (Mum's older sister, who brought her up, had a mantra: "We should never have left the farm.")

These days, if I pass through my home town, it feels like the Hutt left me rather than the other way around. In 1986 one of the first Australian supermalls swallowed our childhood: the houses and backyards where we played with friends who lived close to the main shopping street. The Queensgate mall quickly killed the economy of High Street, for decades the scene of bustling late-night shopping and, in the early 1950s, nefarious teenage meetings in milk bars that featured in the 1954 Mazengarb Report into juvenile delinquency. Lower Hutt — once justifiably celebrated as a "garden city", designed around a striking array of modernist public buildings — is now reconfigured to flow traffic freely to a multi-storey carpark.

Part of the problem of Lower Hutt's CBD is that, as in

Hamilton, early shopkeepers turned their backs on the town's greatest asset: the river that runs alongside the main street. As Mark Twain understood, rivers bring towns much of their colour and life, but the pragmatic need to avoid floods was more pertinent to the European settlers just off Edward Gibbon Wakefield's boats. So an "eastern bank" of shops and pubs enjoying the setting sun never occurred to them: instead there is a formidable stop bank accompanying the river all the way to Petone, where it meets Wellington Harbour.

When Wakefield's immigrants arrived at the Pito-one foreshore in 1840, they hoped to find meadows where flocks might roam, or at least arable land. Instead their view was of dense bush teeming with birdlife, and swamps made impenetrable by giant flax; the river was navigable only by waka and fat eels. This was bounteous territory for those who knew to take what you need and leave the rest. For centuries it had been fought over and settled by iwi, coming all the way from Taranaki, the East Coast, Wairarapa and the South Island.

‘The process is called wool scouring, and in practice it is as ugly as it sounds. To get the grease out of a fleece involves plenty of hot water, and detergent that could almost wash a fly-blown carcass.’

When I first looked over the Petone delta, as a child in the early 1960s, no one was yet singing the blues about the appalling pollution. From the stop bank the immediate view was of rusty 40-gallon drums, and the scum from battery acid, detergent, oils and heavy metals. This was not the mouth of a great waterway, or even the armpit of a windy harbour: this was the anal cleft of the Hutt Valley.

Guilty in all of this were firms that boomed in the 1950s and '60s: effluent flowed into the harbour from the Gear meat works, and many other factories manufacturing batteries, soap, detergents, glue, and industrial chemicals. And my family was no innocent party. The reason I stood so often on the stop bank is that for 70 years that section of the river is where we were in the business of washing wool. The process is called wool scouring, and in practice it is as ugly as it sounds. To get the grease out of a fleece involves plenty of hot water, and detergent that could almost wash a fly-blown carcass. The vocabulary of a wool-scouring flow chart is full of words such as "sludge", "purge" and "heavy solids". One positive by-product is lanolin, which makes wool classers' hands as soft as a baby's. The grease itself — and the crushed dags — can be sold, but some by-products don't bear thinking about.

No one did, until the early 1970s when increased environmental awareness led to law changes. No longer could the factories at the southern end of the Hutt River discharge their toxic waste just before the tide went out in the hope that it would reach Cook Strait rather than Oriental Parade. The DSIR — a few hundred yards away from the wool scour — helped design a filtration system, and when all cisterns were go a television news crew turned up from the NZBC to interview my dad.

This spot in Moerā — a riverside, railway-house suburb — was Wellington's equivalent of "Cancer Alley", the industrial end of the Mississippi River between Baton Rouge and New Orleans. But to me it was a place of excitement.

Inside the large concrete shed we called The Works were towers of wool bales and a labyrinth of machinery, which we clambered over every Saturday morning while our father caught up on paperwork. The plant was full of wonder, with steep ladders and gantries that took you up and over the steaming washing bath, above which hung huge mechanised combs to pull the wool through. It seemed like the nuclear reactor room from the climax of a Bond film, ready to blow. After a tour of the bales stencilled with their exotic destinations — Rotterdam, Liverpool, Genoa, Vladivostok — I migrated to an office, where I enjoyed stabbing at an Imperial typewriter from the 1930s. Everything was covered by a film of grease and fibre.

It was a place built for the imagination of small boys, and the view from the stop bank, looking over at Shannon golf course and the much bigger and uglier factories on the other side of the Hutt River, would have inspired Tom Sawyer. It was a destination full of possibilities, and I was then unaware of its past. The history of the beleaguered end of the Hutt River includes floods that left silt high in the native trees, and a rich ecosystem of birds, insects and worms, all lost after the arrival of the European. I missed the wartime concert of the Artie Shaw big band that took place over the road at Hutt Park — the original home of Wellington Racing Club, before it shifted to Trentham — and never heard the *Lever Hit Parade*, which was sponsored by the soap factory that belched on the horizon. But I did meet Walter Nash at a charity fair near the foreshore.

This polluted Shangri La was on my mind when, one morning in the winter of 1963 — aged three and a half — I put on Dad's heavy, pre-war, lace-up gumboots, got on my hand-me-down trike and left home to go to The Works. It was an epic three-kilometre ride from Waterloo to Moerā, which required negotiating a few intersections and crossing several main roads. The route, memorised while standing on the back seat of the family car, passed along Penrose Street and Ludlam Crescent, two of Lower Hutt's lushest avenues, before traversing a railway bridge into Moerā: "Struggle Town". I didn't pause at the top to see in the distance the Norfolk Pine planted by my grandfather 50 years earlier (which still stands). Instead I hurtled down the other side; with the pedals out of control I diagonally shot across Randwick Road, just getting the handbrake on before hitting the footpath. Traffic was light in 1963, so luckily there was no collision with a Hillman Minx or a Vauxhall Velox.

The Works was in smelling distance now — such a comforting smell, lanolin — and when I got there I parked my chain bike on the gravel beside Dad's old Rover 90 and strode into his office. He was in the middle of a meeting with two Russian wool buyers, and now that I have a three-year-old I can hear the word he would have uttered under his breath.

He apologised to the Russians for the interruption and, before putting the bike in the boot of his car to take me home, phoned Mum with his idea of a joke.

"Have you seen Chris?"

Chris Bourke holds a certificate in sheep shearing awarded by the Wool Board. This confirms he was able — in 1978 — to shear a sheep satisfactorily; the time taken was not relevant at the beginner's level. He then moved to the end of the animal's life cycle, working on the chain gang at Petone's Gear meat works the summer that Hutt Valley contemporary Jon Stevens had No. 1 hits with "Jezebel" and "Montego Bay". His job was to toss sheep skulls into a chute. He is the author of Blue Smoke: the Lost Dawn of New Zealand Popular Music, 1918–1964 *(AUP, 2010).*

Chris Bourke and one of his getaway vehicles.

Alexis Pritchard

Hangdog Campground

I am a dreadful companion on long drives but despite this, my husband Cam and I have driven all over New Zealand in the past 13 years. He is always in the driver's seat making sure he gets me (us) to our destination unharmed and I have passed most of the time sleeping in the seat beside him. Whether we are driving from Auckland to Hamilton or Tākaka, I sleep. In my mind I reach my destination quicker. It also means I avoid the nauseating feelings associated with car sickness.

Now if there was ever a hill to sleep on it is Tākaka Hill. If one is driving to Tākaka from Picton through Nelson and the rest of Tasman Bay you have no choice but to take State Highway 60 which winds its way over and around the flanks of Tākaka Hill. The going is slow and can be sketchy with all its twists and turns.

It is always a relief when I wake up at the bottom of the hill, for two reasons: one, I won't feel sick and two, our final destination, the small laid-back town of Tākaka and Hangdog Campground, the unofficial official climbers' campground, are only 15 minutes away.

Timing is everything when it comes to securing a spot at Hangdog. No bookings. First in gets to claim some land and set up their tent. When all possible space has been claimed the "Fully Full" sign comes out. So we always drive up the driveway with our fingers crossed hoping that once again we have timed it right. Since Cam and I have been venturing down there together, our timing has not let us down.

We discovered that the campground was very basic. A lean-to kitchen area where some campers cooked, an open air sink with cold water to wash your dishes. One hot shower which was not included in your initial site rental. It worked on an honesty policy — you paid $1 per hot shower at the end of your stay. Whether you were fortunate enough to actually get a hot shower was left up to the universe to decide. Many just strolled down to the swimming hole across the road for a dip. There were two toilets with a message on the wall behind the cisterns which I will never forget: "If it's yellow let it mellow if it's brown flush it down."

The attraction of Hangdog for me is that it is simple and uncomplicated. The people you meet there are from all around the world and we are all on the same mission, to climb. No matter your level of expertise, we are all slaves to the rock.

I would get really cold at night. Especially the years we took the blow-up mattress instead of the thick padded and slightly fancier camping mattress. I would go to sleep in a full tracksuit and beanie with two duvets on top of me.

Every morning Cam and I would negotiate who was getting out of our warm bed, to walk over to the tap on the other side of the campground to get water for the first coffee of the day. Mornings at Hangdog were quiet and most campers would be up late at night sitting around the central camp fire listening to fellow campers play the guitar or talking, rehashing the climbs of the day, the triumphs and defeats. Watching climbers talk about a particular climb is fascinating, especially when they get to the crux of a route. They relive every move with their bodies, their hands are holding onto the imaginary rock and their entire bodies shift and the hands change position with every new move as if they are still on the wall. Cam and I and a few other early risers would have this silent time to ourselves to just be.

> **'The attraction of Hangdog for me is that it is simple and uncomplicated. The people you meet there are from all around the world and we are all on the same mission, to climb. No matter your level of expertise, we are all slaves to the rock.'**

Paynes Ford Scenic Reserve, with its diverse and ample limestone crags, is a short walk from the campground. Some days we hopped on the old rickety bikes with wonky steering they had stored next to the recycling area.

I smile fondly when I think of the times there was only one bike left but one of us didn't feel like walking so I would sit on the handle bars laughing all the way to the crag while Cam tried to steer and keep us upright. It's an example of how just being in that place allowed us to be present in the moment and not think about anything other than what we were doing — which was basically letting go and acting like kids at play.

Paynes Ford is west facing so gets the afternoon sun. A lot of the climbing routes are exposed, so during the hotter summer months our routine is dictated by nature.

We all get into a rhythm: morning climbs, back for lunch, a lay in the afternoon sun at the swimming hole and back to rock late afternoon to get a few more climbs in and we make our way back to Hangdog at dusk for dinner.

This place is where I fell in love with rock climbing and the climbing community. Even if you are a seasonal climber like me you are accepted, no questions asked. There are no egos — there is just us and the rock. We celebrate each clean ascent of a route as one, whether it is a grade 18 or a grade 28.

I admire the patience and encouragement of the belayers when their climbing partners are working a climb, figuring out the nuts and bolts. I love the determination and persistence of those on the rock who are up there solving the puzzle on how to get up a slab of rock that to many may seem impossible.

These are my memories of our time in Tākaka during the summers of 05/06, 07/08 and 09/10. It is definitely time for me to return to this wonderful place and make some new ones.

Alexis Pritchard has a BSc in Sports Science from Auckland University and a BHSc in Physiotherapy from Auckland University of Technology. She stumbled upon boxing at the age of 19 and has been fighting like a girl since 2003. She fought at the 2012 Olympics (the first time women's boxing was included at the Games), becoming the first woman to win a bout at the Olympics for New Zealand and scoring the first Olympic boxing win for New Zealand in 16 years. Lex is the 1 ranked boxer nationally in her weight class and has been for a total of ten years. Lex is also a director at Pritchard Cooper Physio & Foot Clinic and acts as in-house physio at Wreck Room. She also bakes and decorates amazing cakes (seriously), is a scrapbooker from way back, and finds it mildly difficult to write about herself in the third person. Her friends are her family.

Rock climbing at Hangdog.

Jarrod Gilbert

Riwaka River

These days the initiation has changed and become more elaborate: it involves poetry, a mask made of a beer box so the pourer has anonymity, and the Mout has a swish of vodka to give it some backbone.

The finest place in New Zealand slopes up the southern bank of a clean, gently flowing river that opens out to an estuary. It gets very hot in summer. There is a tiny island just off the beach. At low tide, you can walk to it. The whole place is beautiful and tranquil.

We simply call it the Riverbank. We gather there every summer from all over the world like it's an imbedded migratory pattern.

There is a small core of us, but any given year numbers can swell as high as 20. There's the Sheriff, of course, the Chairman, he owns the place, the Captain, a legendary figure on the riverbank, the Sergeant at Arms, the Fire Warden, and the Secretary. I'm the CEO. Of the titles I hold or have won, this is the most prestigious.

The road to the Riverbank is gravel and winds past the house and then through rows of kiwifruit. By the time you see the river the outside world no longer exists, you forget all of your troubles. That's the result of what medical practitioners call "blackouts".

It's difficult to put an exact date on when the Riverbank started, but the source of the river is clear. That's because it's signposted. And it's called the Source. It's a tourist thing. The water emerges from a large underground cave at the base of Tākaka Hill. It has spent eons seeping through limestone; it's as clean water as you'll find anywhere. By the time it flows past us in great volumes it's been merely minutes above ground. It's a tad frigid. Common wisdom dictates that it's best to be drunk when you swim.

That cool water first touched my skin when I was 20. I'd become delightfully lost on a road trip and I bumped into some people I recognised from university. That night I was initiated.

The initiation has what one might call a rather primitive foundation, based largely around Old Mout fortified wine. The 18 per cent alcohol was consumed from a large glass jar; the classiest among us did it in one hit. Before wowsers raised the excise tax on cheap plonk and reduced Old Mout to a respectable cider, it was a medicine that cured sanity with madness. It was a drink favoured by homeless men, cash-strapped teenaged boys and the Riverbank.

Riwaka River: with mayhem not occurring.

'**It's difficult to put an exact date on when the Riverbank started, but the source of the river is clear. That's because it's signposted. And it's called the Source. It's a tourist thing.**'

These days the initiation has become more elaborate, it involves poetry, anonymity provided by a mask made of a beer box and the Mout now needs a swish of vodka to give it some backbone. One year Ainger took the initiation and then drank his wife's too. He didn't recover for two full days.

The first year my lawyer joined me on the Riverbank, the Mout inspired him to place a large propane gas canister on the fire. The subsequent explosion destroyed six camping chairs, set fire to a tree and put a strict ban on explosives until a review scheduled for 2017.

The only thing not to be moved by the shock waves and the galaxy of flying embers was the Obelix-like stone, the size of three footballs, which is half buried in the ground on the edge of the fire. It is the rock upon which all activity on the Riverbank rotates. Every night we return to it. It is ancient and wise. The tree above it has grown and broken over the years casting various shadows but the stone has not changed. When we leave, it cools down, but it misses the laughter and is quiet and lonely.

One night the stone bit Spook.

Retiring to his tent he was a little unsteady on his feet and he fell on the fire. A big man, Spook had some trouble removing himself from his unfortunate predicament. For a recklessly long time he flailed around on his back as a turtle does when flipped. Eventually, he hauled his body to the side, rolling his legs over that large smooth stone baked hot by the flames, which peeled the skin off his calf like it was an overripe grape.

We called a meeting. What had we done to anger the stone? Long and hard we thought about this, as did the doctor who examined Spook. He thought it strange that we concerned ourselves with superficial burns and hadn't discovered the dislocated elbow. It was the stone, we said. It was the stone.

We considered putting a complete ban on people falling in the fire after that, but the idea was eventually dropped as being unworkable.

The madness that comes out at night creates stories for the Riverbank, but it is the days when the joy peaks. The days when the sun bakes down on bodies that skip between sanctuaries of shade. Friends catch up. Feet are in the shallows. Cricket bats waft in lazy arcs. Everything moves slowly like the river because nothing has reason to move fast.

Every year we put a leaner at the entrance to the estuary when the water is low. The last one to flee the rushing incoming tide wins a pyrrhic, near-death victory. While we wait we put two crabs on the middle of the table. If one scurries toward your vessel you must consume its contents. If both seek the shelter of your vessel then you nominate somebody else to down theirs. Once the crabs have done a few rounds we get new ones. Those crabs are important players, and must be protected. Besides, the kids, the next generation of Riverbankers, collect new ones for us all the while slowly learning the Riverbank rules. One year while playing crabs, Hoolio got dared to run up a nearby hill and back in 30 minutes. Fuelled by Old Mout he did it in 29.

Old Mout has also been responsible for the creation of many novelty dives. Of all the dives invented at the Riverbank, the sideways dead dog has become the classic. Hours have been spent leaping in and out of the river in the pursuit of its perfection.

But the greatest event on the Riverbank is the New Year's Day wine tour that snakes around the property stopping at various places: the beachfront, the pergola, the pond, the swimming hole and at each stop we enjoy different wines. One year the secretary upped the ante and undertook Edward Wine Hands. That didn't end well and thus entered Riverbank folklore.

Fred Dagg immortalised the words, "We don't know how lucky we are," and for a week or so every year on the Riverbank that sentiment rings true. The only cause for complaint is a jandal blow-out or the Black Caps suffering a batting collapse. I share a drink and a yarn with mates who were just kids when I first arrived there, and now I watch kids growing up. And yet those of us who are the originals seem to act no older. It is the magic of the place; time moves like the river but we age like the stone.

Dr Jarrod Gilbert is a sociologist at the University of Canterbury and the Lead Researcher at Independent Research Solutions. He is the author of the award-winning and best-selling book Patched: the History of Gangs in New Zealand. *In 2015 he won a Canon Media Award as blogger of the year and he currently writes a column for* The New Zealand Herald.

Jarrod Gilbert in a rare contemplative waterborne moment.

Wairau Bar Road: childhood lifeline.

Sido Kitchin

Wairau Pa

I knew Wairau Bar Road like the back of my hand. At night in my slumber as a little girl, I would take the route along the Wairau River to our school in Spring Creek. I would follow every gentle curve and dip in the road from our place, past the homes of the MacDonalds and the milking shed, beyond the chip factory, past the Staffords', over the cattle stops, past the old school house, on and on, finally crossing the rickety wooden bridge across the Wairau River to Spring Creek and my beloved three-classroom school.

Sometimes, in my sleepy head, I'd look out at the wide green river from the back of the school bus, other times I'd ferociously bike the long road, and more than once the river flooded and I swam the familiar route through swollen brown waters. But best of all was when I'd fly, serenely floating just above the road with the wind in my hair, all the way to school.

Dreams of travelling that road beside the river would follow me for years after we moved from Wairau Pa, in rural Marlborough, in 1978. I'd wake up with a start and find myself in towns and cities far away, and an ache would hit my heart. Dad hung on to "the Pa" long after the family splintered and we shifted north, but he let it go when I was in my early 20s.

A decade later, my brother Matt and I were in a hire car, and took the turn off at Spring Creek — halfway between Blenheim and Picton — crossed the new concrete bridge and followed the windy road to the two-room cottage that was the only place our family of seven lived together. It was a sunny day, and my brother and I took strength from each other as we knocked on the door — looking down at the hip-high handle I once stretched on tippy-toe to reach. I felt so full of certainty and hope as I looked at my big brother and waited for the door to open — we were here to buy our house back. Then I woke up.

Wairau Pa was the first time I experienced the intensity of love and loss. My parents bought the cottage on a couple of acres in 1972. It was before vineyards had covered the plains, and most of the Pa was owned and worked by original Māori farming families. My own family had very little — we were a pretty feral bunch, to be fair — but it was a rich and wonderful childhood. We had the freedom to roam, to disappear, to venture, to live in a world of make-believe. It was a beautiful place as far as the eye could see. We were surrounded by wide plains of yellow and green, the emerald river, the golden Wither Hills in the distance, and in the other direction, the dark, majestic Richmond and Robertson Ranges. I thought it was heaven on earth.

> **'My own family had very little – we were a pretty feral bunch, to be fair – but it was a rich and wonderful childhood. We had the freedom to roam, to disappear, to venture, to live in a world of make-believe. It was a beautiful place as far as the eye could see.'**

The reality for my two young parents — who by 27 had had my brother Matt and me, fostered brothers Taka and Jack, and adopted my little sister Abbie — was probably far from utopia . . . especially with money scarce. By the time I was seven, they had decided to move to two different towns. We five kids went in three directions. It was then I had a recurring nightmare about the Wairau River flooding and breaking the banks. I scrambled on to our roof and waited to be rescued by a helicopter while trees and dead cows floated by.

The Wairau River was a force and a constant. Across the road from the house was a stop bank. Climb over the bank and beyond the poplar trees, where our huts sat up high, the Wairau River ran strongly towards the sea.

I learnt to swim in the river. I remember the day I first floated on my back, looking up as the sun shone down on me and my brothers and Dad laughed and yelled with happiness.

Not many people came down to the Pa, unless they lived there. But in the whitebait season, at night we'd wait for car headlights to light up our bedroom walls. My brother Jack had the great plan for us to wrap up in blankets and wait in the long grass on the side of the road in the dark of night. I can still remember the look of shock on the face of a woman sitting in a passenger seat when she saw five naked kids jump out and flash her.

I'll also never forget the whitebait fritters Aunty Lou Stafford made. They were so fat, packed with whitebait, and I'd sit there and sob as I was told to eat up — it was the little black eyes I couldn't handle. If only . . .

The week before the moving truck came, I wallpapered the bedroom I shared with my four siblings with my precious greeting card collection, sticking pins and tape everywhere I could. But when I saw the piano going into the truck, I realised my plan had failed. The pain was unforgettable.

There were plenty of visits to Wairau Pa over the years that followed, but they were always tinged with sadness. The place got more and more beautiful, but it was hard to find the joy . . . because from the moment we arrived, I knew we would have to leave for somewhere that could never compare. The day I tried to run up and take my normal flying route to the washing line and didn't get lift-off will go down in family history as the day I finally cracked. Oh, how I wept. Wairau Pa was my childhood and it was over.

Dad took me for my first driving lesson along the familiar road, and I sobbed the whole way.

Last time I drove down to the Pa, I came around the bend and spotted the roof of the house surrounded by the fruit trees Mum planted and the field which gave us the crops which fed us through the seasons. I slowed the car but I couldn't stop. Instead I drove to the end of Wairau Bar Road and walked along the boulder bank where the mighty river finally collides with the sea. This is one of the most important ancient sites in New Zealand — where the very first Māori settled in the 1300s, and where giant moa once roamed. You can feel how special it is.

Sido Kitchin stops to smell the flowers.

I looked back at the sunlight kissing the Wither Hills, the big blue skies and the river running to the sea. It was a hot and sunny Marlborough day, but right here it was wild and windy — it always is — and the perfect place to howl.

It has better to have loved and lost, then never have loved at all. But it still hurts like hell.

Sido Kitchin is a journalist, currently Editor-in-Chief of popular magazines Woman's Day *and* New Zealand Woman's Weekly. *Following in the footsteps of her newspaper journo father and brother, Sido began working in media aged 18. She has worked in newspapers, magazines and television publicity here and in Australia. Sido lives in Auckland with her husband Conrad Armstrong and two children, Cleo and Darcy.*

Lower Dashwood, Awatere Valley: an experiment in nature.

Erica Crawford

Lower Dashwood, Awatere Valley

Perhaps because I'm not from New Zealand, the place I care about is one I'm in the process of creating — or re-creating. It's the raw material of a vision, and my husband, Kim, and I have owned it for 10 years.

It's one of our Loveblock vineyards off State Highway 1 in Marlborough, where it cleaves down to Seddon. From the site you can see across to Wellington in one direction, and to hills and away to salt pans in the other direction.

We got it in 2006, simply because it is so amazing. It's actually a stupid place to plant grapes, but that didn't stop us.

Water is like gold down there. But we already owned part of this property and some other property down the road. We had just sold Kim Crawford Wines, we felt ten feet tall and bullet proof. So when it came up, the question was not why should we buy it, but why wouldn't we?

We might have got better advice if we'd asked for it, but we probably wouldn't have taken it.

On different days it looks so different but it's always breathtaking. And it's quiet — sometimes you can hear the drip, drip, drip of the irrigation system bringing precious water to the vines.

It's certified organic now, but it wasn't when we got it. The soil was very depleted and we had to do a lot of work on it.

We have had to learn so much on the run. We follow the old Hebrew agricultural philosophy of shmita, or summer fallow, letting the land rest every seven years. We need that to keep improving the soil, which is largely clay and probably some of the worst in Marlborough. We've got to get the soil biology activated, so we are planting things like lucerne to improve the structure of the soil.

We were so ambitious with our first plantings and half of them didn't work out. There's probably a reason why no one's planted grapes on soil exactly like ours before.

It's called wither soil. But one thing that thrives in this terrain and in the face of the terrible winds we get is the bronze beetle. That was the thing that really stumped us.

They come out at 20 minutes past sunset every day. They copulate for two hours, eat for three hours, then fall down and lay their eggs. They've caused tremendous damage.

Because we're surrounded by pastureland, there are a lot of them, but we didn't know this, so we planted vineyards in their path with disastrous results.

But at the same time, because the soil is so different and because the area is so cold, so exposed, so windy — when you do get something from it, it's exquisite.

> ❛But at the same time, because the soil is so different and because the area is so cold, so exposed, so windy – when you do get something from it, it's exquisite.❜

We have started to put beef cattle on the property as well, because I don't think a single crop is a good thing, and I want to do "Loveblock-certified organic grass-fed beef".

We're firmly rooted in the area, even though we live in Auckland. I spend several days a week here. For me it's about the organic farm. Growing grapes organically is quite different. I'm doing a viticulture degree because I need to know how to do things properly.

What we see in Marlborough — especially here in the Awatere Valley where big companies are planting 200-hectare blocks — is that everything is becoming so automated. Hands don't even touch the grapes much any more. We're going in the opposite direction.

Sadly, no one's interested in experimenting and trying new ways of doing things. All they grow is sauvignon blanc, because that's what the world wants to buy.

For us it's more about an idea. Eventually I'd like to get to the point where you can feed people entirely from one place, a bit like River Cottage. It's a long way off and again it's more of a struggle than I foresaw. We had a little vege garden, which went by the wayside because it's just not easy to grow that sort of stuff. But we're starting that again.

The staff have some cattle on the land and did a successful cull a few months ago. Also we need the cows to eat grass.

We don't have much in the way of buildings. There's an old manor house nearby from the original owners of the property, but someone else owns that part of the land now. Instead we have a shearing shed that we use as an office cum smoko room cum everything else.

There's no accommodation. For that we have to apply for consent to build up and have a little flat. At the moment we stay with other people. That's not ideal — you need to go to sleep and wake up in a place to belong there.

But I love it so much I don't care. And everyone else is the same. People who work in these places are different. They don't just work there because it's a job, they work there because it's a philosophy.

We are surrounded by big players who do things differently from us, but we are all part of a community and work together.

Some sweet things have happened as a result. The New Zealand falcon is badly depleted but there are a few in the valley. They made a nest on our farm. We get little frozen chickens delivered to Mel and she puts them out on a platform and the falcons swoop down and carry them off to eat.

We will never run out of things to learn or to experiment with. We could have done here what we did before with Kim Crawford Wines and made a lot of money again, but it would have just been the same old process. What story would we have had to tell?

Purpose is important. Kim's mother is a good example of that. She's 89 and she's just been to look after her grandchildren on a farm in Canterbury. She did a road trip to Mexico last year. It's so important not to get bored as you get older. A lot of people drink too much — and boredom is one of the main reasons.

Whatever else this property yields, it will give us 10 years of not being bored.

Erica Crawford started her career as a young scientist in cardiac medicine in her native South Africa, but it was her self-taught skills as an exporter and marketer that saw her rise to business prominence in New Zealand. Erica co-founded Kim Crawford Wines in 1996, and in a unique deal, the brand and IP was sold after some seven years. The bulk of Erica's time is now spent on her own new wine venture and management of the family's wine interests. Organic farming is at the heart of the operations, a deeply held philosophy that she is now fortunate to "live" on a daily basis.

Erica Crawford: a new purpose.

Arthur Baysting

Tiromoana

I grew up in Nelson and long before I visited the West Coast I knew it from my father's slide shows. He worked for the Forest Service and drove his yellow Bedford truck on regular trips down there to teach trainees about fire safety and first aid. Along the coast road he'd often stop and take scenic photographs. I would have been 11 or 12 at the time and remember seeing an island, looking like a gigantic fish pursuing what I imagined were rock spirits.

In the mid-1970s, my partner, Jean Clarkson, and I were part of a group of a dozen young people wanting to buy a piece of communal land. We were the Woodstock generation and we thought of ourselves as alternative life-stylers although to many we were "hippies" and "greenies". In those days those terms were often used as swear words. We'd been looking north of Auckland and in the Coromandel but somehow we settled for a block at Tiromoana at the mouth of the Fox (Potikohua) River.

When we went down to our land, I was amazed to see the island was right there, just over the road. At low tide we could easily walk across to Seal Island and explore it. There was even a hut on it, shelter for crayfishers and anyone caught by the tide. Amazingly, for the tempestuous West Coast, the wide sheltered beach made it safe for swimming.

We discovered the block we'd purchased was bigger than we realised. The coastal boundary on State Highway 6 ran for more than a kilometre up to the mouth of the Fox then stretched another kilometre and a half more along the limestone cliffs above the river, into what is now the Paparoa National Park.

I still haven't got used to the scale of the place. Everything is so huge that humans are reduced to dots in the landscape. It rains a bit — it is, after all, a rainforest — but the warm ocean current that creates the sub-tropical microclimate means the rain isn't cold, and just as often there are beautiful blue-sky days. Walking in the bush among the weird limestone formations I still feel spirits, real or imagined. On clear nights I look up and marvel at the thickest, fattest, most bejewelled Milky Way I've ever seen.

After buying the land, we all chipped in a bit more and built a house that's been a family home ever since. Jean and I lived there for several months in the late 1970s and in those early days the district wasn't hooked up to the grid. It meant hard labour for the women who did the cooking and the washing and brought up the babies, while the men were off doing whatever it was that the men did.

Tiromoana: communal land for the Woodstock generation.

For me that often meant looking for songs. I can't explain why, but from my first visit down there, songs were somehow easier to find. I was a novice songwriter and I invited musician friends down to stay. We rarely came away without something interesting.

One stormy night I woke to the sound of distant cannon. I followed the sound along the road and found myself looking down at an ocean-churning full tide. The loud cracking sounds were from under the sea where large boulders were being pounded against each other. It was rock music, but not as I knew it.

There's a rocky tunnel on our land, just where the old wooden road bridge runs into our block. Before it was built Cobb & Co. dynamited a hole through the rock wide enough for their big open Cadillacs to drive through and along the bank to a shallower, safe crossing. In the 1960s they built a flash new bridge and were about to demolish the old one when the locals formed a Bridge Preservation Group and saved the day. It used to be where they had the summer Saturday markets but now they've shifted to Katajuta on the north bank. Our neighbours were here before we came, hippier hippies than us, with a geodesic dome to prove it.

> **'One stormy night I woke to the sound of distant cannon. I followed the sound along the road and found myself looking down at an ocean-churning full tide.'**

We went down to Tiromoana to celebrate my 50th birthday. We swam in the sea and waded across the freezing river. The next day we set out to conquer the hill on our land, sometimes referred to as Mount Bastard. I was told that if I lost the track it might mean trouble. Of course, I did just that and the expedition turned into a tortuous bush-bashing epic that took six or seven hours to get to the top and back down. From the summit we could clearly see Aorangi Mount Cook but the view failed to impress our children, James and Rosie. The challenging rock-climbing and the scratched arms and legs they suffered have become part of family legend.

It is an unbelievable place. With nīkau forests and their stone phantoms, it's true Craig Potton country and up river in the National Park you're in landscapes that feel unchanged for centuries. There's also the Fox River caving system, where I once ventured. The eerie blackness was too spooky for me and I haven't been back.

The Fox River mouth has its own history. A hundred and fifty years ago a gold strike saw the town of Brighton appear virtually overnight, with 6000 people, 23 hotels, five brothels and a theatre. Within three years the gold was gone so the miners dismantled the town and moved everything on to the next discovery.

The mouth of the Fox is where Geoff Murphy and Bruno Lawrence made Blerta's *Wild Man* movie. More recently Peter Jackson used CGI'd views of the limestone cliffs for Rivendell in *LOTR*, and just down the way Gaylene Preston filmed *Perfect Strangers*. Eleanor Catton's Man Booker Prize-winner *The Luminaries* has been a key event in the cultural transformation of the Coast. Literary tourists visit Hokitika and many also check out Denniston, north of Westport, the setting for Jenny Pattrick's best seller *Denniston Rose*.

Writers, craftspeople, film-makers and musicians make up a good proportion of the people living along SH6. The isolation and the sub-tropical climate have helped make it a kind of cultural sanctuary. Spiritual home for the musicians is the legendary Barrytown Hall. Townes van Zandt famously played here, and it's regarded by international indie artists as a great gig, as it is for up and coming New Zealand bands. Lately the locals have fixed it up, repiling it and putting in flash plumbing, in recognition of its unique place in our musical history.

Nowadays tourism is the new go, and all along the coast are Airbnbs and "glamping" sites. Over the past 10 years the number of visitors has doubled and official DOC figures show that in 2015 there were more than 500,000 tourists at Punakāiki.

At Tiro we barely notice them. In their cars and camper vans the Pancake Rock pilgrims sound like bumble bees buzzing past in the distance. Bikers come from all over. With the wild scenery and the ocean, SH6 is seen as one of the most beautiful rides in the world.

The West Coast doesn't always rate with the rest of New Zealand. Television's view of it is often job lay-offs, Cave Creek or Pike River, with a touch of Appalachia. The truth is that Coasters are a breed apart: generous and stoic, with a sense of humour that's bone dry and often laugh-out-loud funny. And they know how to party.

At Easter 2014 Jean and I and our friend Bill Lake went down to celebrate a neighbour's anniversary. We'd booked on the TranzAlpine from Christchurch, but the train was cancelled due to heavy snow. So was the Railways bus. We drove over and found a lot of old friends had turned up. It rained and the electricity went down, but a couple of generators were soon sparked up and the band played on. Someone dropped by later and said a few roofs had been blown off in Westport and a tornado had obliterated the Greymouth Band Hall. Then we heard that further south a truck and trailer unit had been rolled over by the wind.

Later we discovered that ex-cyclone Ita had roared down out of the Pacific and felled an estimated 20,000ha of forest. Much of it was rimu and tōtara, some 800 to 1000 years old, and whole stands of mature trees had their trunks snapped off above the ground. Up the Fox River, the Inland Pack Track to Punakāiki was — and still is — impassable. Full-size trees lie across the track, piled up like pick-up sticks. Nobody died but it was the Coast's worst storm in living memory.

Writing this piece made me realise the influence that Tiro has had on our lives. It's meant enduring friendships with the people we bought the land with. And it's been a place of peace and solitude away from the rest of the world. At Tiro in 1978, Fane Flaws and I wrote a song called "Tears" that became well-known. This allowed me to convince myself I was a songwriter and since then it's given me a few other lucky ones. Through them I've had a career in the music industry, meeting amazing people and travelling to wondrous places around the globe. If I hadn't found that first song none of this would have happened.

Tony Backhouse and I wrote another one down at Tiro. Thirty years on, a gospel choir in Australia is still singing it.

> I can feel All of Heaven
> Raining down on me.

Arthur Baysting lives in Grey Lynn with his partner, the artist Jean Clarkson. He has worked as a health researcher, journalist, scriptwriter, film-maker and stand-up comedian. He writes songs and children's books with the Australian entertainer Justine Clarke and collaborates with Peter Dasent, Bill Lake, Nick Bollinger and others on various music and writing projects. He worked for a number of years with Mike Chunn, including helping to introduce ukuleles into New Zealand schools. His interests range from children's health to popular culture.

Arthur Baysting: songs were easier to find.

Blaketown: not a seaside suburb.

Kate De Goldi

Blaketown

Blaketown, Greymouth is beside the beach, but I doubt anyone has ever thought of it as a seaside suburb. The "seaside" concept, with its historic codings — piers, leisurely strolls, ice cream, sandcastles — doesn't work for West Coast shorelines. And besides, Blaketown — a weathered, largely treeless, working-class suburb — more or less has its back to the beach. The Tasman Sea is always *there,* growling in the background, but the beach is somehow detached from the suburb. It's nearly always empty — a bleak, stony, scoured stretch of coast south of the breakwater at the mouth of the Grey River. The sea is heaving and inhospitable and noisy, the stones ceaselessly sucked and dumped with great clatter. No swimming, here. No turning your back on the Tasman either, as our Uncle Toni once warned us. *Surf Guide* describes the waves as *fast, punchy, powerful, hollow,* a good bunch of adjectives for a body of water whose breakers seem generally to snarl.

Teenagers have always been faithful — there are usually used condoms around the tideline — the long hillocks of stone and driftwood provide a rough shelter for love. Decades ago, on a late December afternoon, my boy cousins filched wine from our grandparents' fiftieth wedding anniversary party and got memorably drunk down in the stony hollows. Sometimes, during a big sea, an audience might gather to watch the Grey River bar surging between Cobden and Greymouth. And there are usually a few dedicated fishermen up at the tiphead. But mostly the town stays away. Once, a friend of mine, incredulous at my pleasure in the place, described Blaketown and its shoreline as possibly the arsehole of the universe.

I don't see it. Or rather, though my adult self sees the austerity of the coastline, hears the sea's fury and knows well the treacherous conditions under which fishermen work those waters, my true sense of the place was encoded quite differently years ago — across the 15 childhood summers our family stayed in Blaketown with our grandparents. These were heavily ritualised holidays, beginning with the journey across the Alps, the stops throughout the Taramakau Valley at various relations', the arrival at 4 Reid Street where, always, our father would get out of the car, stretch, take a deep breath and say with evident pleasure, "Smell *that!*"

Coal smoke, salt air, sea grass, hot gravel. The very particular smells of our grandparents' home and their persons. Cicadas. Rust. Date pits drying along the window sill. Brackish drinking water. A sleepy afternoon by the coal range. The clunk of the oven door, the shovel scratching in the coal bucket. This sensory mash was a beguiling contrast to the sounds and smells and sights of our Christchurch life. Blaketown time was thoroughly *other* — it was the Coast, after all, Canterbury's dark twin, but also, our grandparents were Italian and like no one else in our lives — exotic, beloved, and always a little mysterious.

> **❝Cicadas. Rust. Date pits drying along the window sill. Brackish drinking water. A sleepy afternoon by the coal range.❞**

Curiously, in my interior slide show of those summers — sharp images in the saturated colours of the 1960s and '70s — I can never quite locate our mother, though she was certainly there — cooking, helping, talking for long hours with our grandmother, marking time perhaps. But I think this "absence" points up a significant aspect of our Blaketown episodes: there my sisters and I inhabited a kind of parallel but subtly separate world, a heightened, imaginatively charged universe in which the usual powerful norms (our mother, primarily) receded and became unimportant. And the storybook quality of our grandparents, elderly, bent, kindly but enigmatic, with heavy accents and quaint habits, amplified this perception.

There were two stage sets in this altered world: the interior of 4 Reid Street; the suburb and the beach. Inside, we slept in double beds, sat on the same benches at the table our three aunts had once occupied, and closely studied every aspect of the house and its ornamentation — this iconography a kind of lens on our grandparents' hidden selves and our father's life before us. Outside the house we roamed the Blaketown streets, charmed by every particular — the grass, the houses, the guttering, the colour of the footpaths, the seaside plantings, the rusting machinery around the lagoon, the rusting playground equipment, the strong feeling that everything hovered at the edge of wildness — except the beach where the wild had won and the scene was operatic.

It amazes me now to think of our unsupervised play at that beach. We took food so there was no need to return to the house and our parents came down only occasionally. So the great expanse of stone and sand, dried kelp, fish remnants, sodden logs, the sour smelling dune grass — all became our playground, sans adults and pesky instruction. We spent hours and hours absorbed in one elaborate narrative or another, crouching behind logs, slogging purposefully up the beach, climbing the huge slabs of hewn rock around the tiphead — a frankly dangerous undertaking which makes me shudder now.

My sisters and I used to play with *stones*, I told my children once. Blaketown beach stones are greywacke, a very satisfactory size and weight in the hand and often flecked with mica — or gold, as we thought of it. We used the stones in countless games. Or we stacked them, sorted them, carted them home to our grandmother's laundry to wet them again and again so our fool's gold would continue to glint in the sun.

Sometimes we just lay on the warm stones (it was always hot), studying them in their abundance and the shadows between them, choosing favourites, enjoying the feel of their surfaces and shapes. Or we lay on our backs and talked. Stared up at the sky and listened to the crazy sea. Or lay the other way and stared at the 12 apostle hills, counting often to make sure there weren't in fact 13 peaks.

It was our father who told us about the 12 apostles. He told us about the great gouge in the hills from where the huge rock slabs around the tip had been quarried. He told us about shipwrecks along the coastline, coal mining in the Grey Valley, about swimming in the lagoon and building a fire in the stones so he and Toni could boil mussels in a tin or roast a potato. He told us about the West Coast sun setting red and fiery in the sea, about his first race meeting, his sisters' tying him to a fence in a game of cowboys and Indians, his wriggling the fence pale loose and falling flat on his nose, reshaping it forever . . .

As much as our mother faded in Blaketown our father came to the front of the stage. He was always an important presence in our lives, a man who shared much of himself with his daughters, but in Greymouth he was suddenly more there, properly at home now, less a parent preoccupied by demanding work and responsibilities than a much favoured son, visibly relaxed, and even more confidential. We felt his happiness. We loved his stories. Our supercharged Blaketown world had once been his playground and we liked to imagine him, tanned and skinny and spirited, at large in this realm. His pleasure in recalling that old self in his natural habitat, sealed the deal for us, I think. Our own happiness in Blaketown and its beach deepened; everything about it — sea, stones, smell — became totemic, freighted with layers of family relationship and experience, and shot through with the memory of our father's wonder at his good fortune.

Isn't it marvellous? he would say, cross-legged on the stones, gesturing at it all — the sweep of sky and sea, the hills, the brooding tiphead. Nowhere like it.

Yes, yes. Yes.

Kate De Goldi writes fiction for all ages. She has been recipient of The Michael King Fellowship and twice winner of New Zealand Post Children's Book of the Year. Her new novel is From the Cutting Room of Barney Kettle. *Kate reviews books in print and broadcast media and teaches creative writing at schools throughout New Zealand. She is co-editor, with Susan Paris, of* ANNUAL, *a miscellany for 9–12 year olds, which will be published in October 2016.*

Kate De Goldi in poncho with sisters Clare and Margaret Mary on the beach.

Reading Street: home to the Gunns and the Shoots.

Jason Gunn

Reading Street

My cul-de-sac. Reading Street, Ilam in Christchurch.

It's the place that made me who I am.

It's where I learnt to do the things I do.

My cul-de-sac was everything to me.

First and foremost it was a stage. We lived at the end of the street, which meant we were front of stage. And it always did feel like a stage. With the surrounding houses you always had an audience. Mrs Fahey in her kitchen window, Mrs Hills in her garden and Mr Shoot trimming his edges — yes the Gunns and the Shoots lived in the same street — what's the chances?

I'm going to be honest, I loved being out there on show. I mean everything I did on my skateboard, or my bike ... every game of cricket I played, every conversion I kicked was made bigger than it needed to be because ... the world was watching — or at least someone was.

'It was Wembley stadium. It was Broadway. It was the MCG and I was the entire Channel 9 commentary team.'

You were "on" the whole time.
It was Wembley stadium. It was Broadway. It was the MCG and I was the entire Channel 9 commentary team.

We had a such a mix of people in our cul-de-sac. A lot of families. Students. Retired folk. I loved chatting to them all. I loved making them laugh. I loved hearing their stories.

I learnt back then that sure, we're all very different but we've all got a good yarn to tell. We're all passionate about something. We all like to be entertained.

I also learnt there was a time to shut up and go home — something I still need to remind myself today.

Mum would always say, "Go play in the street," — 'cos in those days you did. It wasn't a dangerous place.

She still lives there. And whenever I visit . . . I look down our drive and stare out to the middle, remembering the great times. I'm so very grateful for all that it taught me. All that it enabled me to be.

My cul-de-sac. A dead end? Far from.

Jason Gunn is a New Zealand television presenter, director, writer and radio announcer. He had his first taste of the entertainment industry aged 17, when he was cast in the lead role of Adrian Mole in the touring musical The Secret Diary of Adrian Mole aged 13 3/4. *At 18, he auditioned for a presenting role at TVNZ and soon became the face of New Zealand children's television, with* Jase TV *and the long-running* Son of a Gunn Show. *Jason went on to host many top TV shows including* Dancing with the Stars, *and game shows* The Rich List *and* Wheel of Fortune. *Jason currently co-hosts the nationwide* More FM Drive *show and is launching his own YouTube channel — youtube. com/jasongunn. He and his wife, Janine Morrell-Gunn, run Whitebait Media, a television production and facilities company. They live on a lifestyle block just out of Christchurch, where Jason is still learning how to drive a tractor.*

Jason Gunn in his favourite cul de sac.

Port Hills: a nightmare for anyone with mild hay fever.

Jack Tame

Port Hills

They called us the Farley Brothers.

I dunno why. From memory the name Farley was only relevant 'cos it wasn't relevant, if you get what I mean. It was random before "random" became a teenage thing. Maybe we constructed it as some secretive in-joke and delighted as our parents struggled to decode some non-existent meaning.

I doubt we thought about it that much. I expect Mike simply pitched it up when we were flipping and lolling on the trampoline after school — maybe one of us joked about forming a two-person circus act.

Unlike most self-generated nicknames, the Farley Brothers stuck.

We had Mike's dog, too. Jess. Jesse. We called her Farley Pup and sometimes, when we got worn out between the trampoline after school and brass band rehearsal, we'd construct an obstacle course in Mike's backyard and make *Tux Wonder Dogs* videos. I'd dig out all sorts of shit from Mike's dad's old shed and the ceiling space above the garage: boogie boards, paint cans and plywood planks. I'm not convinced she loved it.

Mike got his licence first. He was young — 15 or 16. His parents bought him a little white Civic hatchback with fold-forward front seats and someone linked a CD player to a couple of dodgy speakers in the back.

We couldn't go far, though. We could never afford much more than 10 bucks worth of gas, and to this day, Mike's Civic is the only car I've ever run dry. We weren't interested in driving to town or hanging around shopping malls. You could do that stuff from the bus. Instead we chased a closer freedom: We picked up Jesse, a half scoop each and a few jam wraps for dessert. The Farley Brothers fled to the hills.

> **'From our rock above the world we could see right down the valley to the water's edge. We could throw stones and boulders without concern. Sometimes we'd make target practice of an old volcanic stone wall that some poor soul likely lifted into place more than a century ago.'**

My parents bought a section high on Huntsbury when I was three or four years old. I can still remember Dad hanging from the timber as he built the place, the massive excavator that carved up the dirt for the foundations of our home.

Our place faced east and the hill dropped off not far beyond our fence into a valley. On a bad day, the easterly cut across the suburbs and straight up our backyard cricket pitch. On a good day, you could trace Pegasus Bay from the New Brighton Pier to the Kaikoura Ranges. From the upstairs bedrooms, we had the trifecta view: the city, the Alps, the sea.

Many visitors to Christchurch are surprised to discover the city has hills. They're unaware that Lyttelton Harbour is in the basin of an extinct volcano. Blame it on the brochures promoting punting and plains; everyone expects everything to be flat.

In some part at least, this is because the Port Hills boast few aesthetic niceties. They are ugly hills: Brown and scraggy and harsh in all seasons and light. They are largely bare of trees, and on the city side the houses stretch unevenly and only part of the way up. Some of the hills are home to scattered livestock and all have plenty of dust. They're a nightmare for anyone with even mild hay fever. And I can recall several occasions during roaring nor' westers, when scrub fires picked up.

Mike and I loved the escape. We'd drive up Cashmere Hill, past the poshest houses to where cyclists wound two abreast up over Dyers Pass. The road isn't steep, but it's long and the corners are tight. Jesse would reach up from my lap and we shared the billowing air.

At the Sign of the Kiwi you could stop for a muffin and admire the view or drop straight over into the harbour and down into Governor's Bay. The Farleys always turned left. The Civic crept by the last tracks of Victoria Park, where serious mountain bikers laced up their body armour and ski goggles, up along the Port Hills' crater rim. From the city and the plains, the Summit Road ridge looked a lonely, exposed place. But for the Farleys it was all escapist joy, wild and windy and silent and with the world at our feet.

We had a spot. A rock. A crusty old chunk of lava.

It was just reachable before our chips were totally cold and we'd always save enough petrol so as not to have to descend the hill afterwards in neutral gear. It was halfway, perhaps, between the very top of Huntsbury Hill and the top of Victoria Park, suspended on a rocky peninsula that cut out East above the harbour. We put Jesse on her lead and skipped from the Civic between the brown tussock and the rocks, to a barbed wire fence on the peninsula ridge. At certain times of year little wisps of grubby wool would catch in the snags, and we'd trace the fence to a point where we could cross without catching our school shorts.

I'd show off. I'd point out the little saddle at Gebbies Pass, where you could just see the spit of land separating Lake Ellesmere and the sea. I'd make Mike squint at Ripapa Island, where Armstrong guns rusted in a secret World War I fort, and where the famed German naval officer Felix von Luckner saw out the war. I'd pontificate on whether Russian or German submarines ever made it this far. I'd linger on Quail Island. A leper colony! A bay of shipwrecks! Both Scott and Shackleton's pre-Antarctic base! I'd imagine the grim climb for Canterbury's first British settlers, up and over the hill to swamplands and graft.

Our chips would be gone, the sad little rip-top tin of tomato sauce left to roll meek and empty in the wind.

From our rock above the world we could see right down the valley to the water's edge. We could throw stones and boulders without concern. Sometimes we'd make target practice of an old volcanic stone wall that some poor soul likely lifted into place more than a century ago.

When our chips were finished, on one of our early visits, I placed a dollar coin in the middle of our perch, as a test of whether anyone else visited. I figured any other adventurers would collect the dollar and what seemed like the Farleys' alone would not actually be all ours. But in years of missions to our spot, no one ever did. Eventually Mike and Jess and I would turn back to the city and the Southern Alps and know it was time to go home.

I went back after the earthquakes. I hadn't been in years.

It was on a run one Christmas, down Huntsbury from the home Dad built and back up Cashmere Hill. As I traced Summit Road along the crater rim, I detoured. I scrambled through the tussock and the rocks to an old fence with brown wool caught in its barbs. Our rock above the world is still there, though many others on the summit ridge came tumbling, terribly, down.

Jess, our sweet Farley Pup has long since died. Mike and I haven't lived in the same city for a decade and we don't keep contact like we should.

That dry summer's afternoon, I was the solitary Farley in our solitary place. Islands, Alps, ocean and plains: the view hasn't changed much in five million years. But you know what? Someone found that dollar.

Jack Tame is a broadcaster and columnist who has reported on US affairs for TVNZ news since 2006. He also hosts the Saturday morning radio show on NewstalkZB and has a weekly column in the Herald on Sunday.

Jack Tame goes the distance.

Paula Ryan

Weedons/Broadfields

A third-generation New Zealander, my forebears were Irish. Great grandfather Sandy Mick Ryan (from rural Tipperary) immigrated to New Zealand with his brother in 1856. He settled in Weedons/Broadfields, just south of Christchurch. I still recall his son (my grandfather, Patrick Francis) as an elderly gentleman in tweed pants, a waistcoat over shirt sleeves, holding a fob watch. He was overseeing (with my father, Francis Patrick) the annual family bacon curing and onion pickling, in a courtyard filled with vats of salt and sugar and two-foot high preserving crocks.

Unfortunately, he died when I was five and I only experienced my other grandparent (Mum's mother) for a few more years, so I missed the interaction with grandparents that I now cherish so much with my own grandchildren.

Dad inherited the 131-hectare mixed cropping farm at Weedons that we called Grasslea, where I was born. I have many fond memories of life on this flat, grassy Canterbury landscape. Much of the Canterbury plains was formerly riverbed but converted over time to farm lands, chosen at that time for mixed cropping and sheep farming.

My parents, being devout Catholics, produced a family of six. I slotted in as second born. Mother clearly had no sense of rhythm as she delivered my youngest sister, Maria, at 49 years of age, but we are delighted as Maria has kept her siblings youthful.

Four daughters and two sons spread over 20 years meant there was much toing and froing from home base. We all attended Weedons Primary School where sport was encouraged by our teacher Wally Wilkinson (an international rugby league referee). We were also encouraged into sporting activities by our mother, who had played hockey for Otago and Wellington for nine years and who had an All Black brother, my uncle, Don Oliver. My specialty was the long jump and chosen team sport . . . hockey. We cycled the five kilometres to school, much of it on a gravel road. The afternoon ride home was often easier, if the nor-wester was up! My brother Oliver often rode the family pony as the school set aside a horse paddock for students.

Higher education opportunities were missed by our parents, so this became a priority for us. Boarding schools for secondary education were essential, and we were encouraged to select our school and later be discerning in our career choices.

I chose Teschemakers in Oamaru, a girls' school run by Dominican nuns. Most pupils were farmers' daughters. My choice was based on the fact that my favourite cousin (also from a south Canterbury farm) was already a boarder. We DCT girls . . . (Dominican College Teschemakers) had much in common and the nuns' discipline did us no harm. We returned home only three times a year, and I couldn't wait to step off the bus for those school holidays. I was a farm girl at heart and enjoyed helping my father lamb the ewes at 5am on frosty mornings during the lambing season. Feeding out was also a favourite experience. So much so, that in later years when I won the Queen of the Furrow title at the World Ploughing Championships, held on a farm nearby, my good friend and prominent New Zealand photographer Euan Sarginson called me Turnips — a name that stuck forever.

❝We indulged them by shucking and serving fresh Bluff oysters by the sack or flipping hearty patties loaded with West Coast whitebait.❞

In those early days on the farm we wanted for nothing. We reared our own mutton, pork, chickens and Muscovy ducks. We grew a large vegetable garden when the word organic wasn't even known. Gooseberries, blackcurrants, apples and Doris plums flourished in abundance. My mother, Nellie, a domestic goddess in her day, made jams, sauces and chutneys just as her forebears had.

At shearing time, the clear Canterbury air became heavy with the perfume of fresh lanolin-smelling fleeces. Good shearers were national heroes then. The women folk on the farm toted baskets of home-baked buttery scones and cream-filled sponges every morning and afternoon to the shearing team at smoko time. The same applied to the hot nor'-west wheat harvesting days, when the preferred thirst-quenching beverages were cold sweet milky tea or home-made ginger beer. The smells of freshly baled hay, new jute sacks and sheep yards still invoke memories.

We had no sense of wealth or poverty. Farm life was simple, natural and by today's standards, healthy. Only Sure-To-Rise baking powder came in a packet and the only recipe book to be seen was the *Edmonds Cook Book*. When Dad killed a hogget, we sat crossed legged, watching him portion it into the various cuts, while fighting over whose turn it was to get the knuckle bones. We ate everything — from the kidneys and liver, to the chops and roast joints. Pigs' trotters and pickled pork bones were my favourite pork dishes and Nellie's brawn was a highlight served with Worcestershire sauce — so much more delicate and less jellied than "what those townies eat".

Sundays were full-on family days. The day started with mass at Lincoln and the Ryans had the front pew, reserved through tradition. I hated that, as we were often late, which meant crawling past a full church. However, one thing is for sure, we were the best dressed of the entire congregation. Mother was a dress-maker by trade and she loved to dress her four daughters like princesses. Fabric from Ballantynes, a stack of Butterick and Vogue pattern books, her Singer sewing machine and she was in sewing heaven. I can't sew a stitch — I never had to, but the fashion seed was well and truly planted.

Eating and drinking occupied most of our Sunday afternoons on the farm. Sunday lunch was the main meal and was always a roast. Our father encouraged intelligent conversation and believed those who think young stay young at heart, so he instigated post-lunch debating and the sharing of humour, which inevitably resulted in some gleeful hilarity. Sadly, unlike that of Oscar Wilde or Dorothy Parker, none of it was ever documented, but the Irish craic and joke-telling has provided lasting memories.

Wine was an oddity then. When Cold Duck was eventually included in the Sunday beverage list, we almost felt European. Sometimes we would remain at the table until 4pm drinking Father's favourite post-lunch tipple — Tia Maria, topped with the leftover cream from dessert, which was inevitably pavlova, trifle or baked Alaska. Nothing came in a box from a supermarket. Everything, and I mean everything, was made from scratch with farm produce. Even the cream was separated from the milk. Yes, we had cows for our domestic dairy consumption. Sometimes Granny (Mother's mum, who lived with us in her dotage) made butter, saltless and delicious, which she served with griddle scones cooked on the open fire. The cow paddock produced the best-tasting pink mushrooms in season, which were collected by the bucketful. When we grew peas for Wattie's, we would pick and pod the sweetest, until Dad realised it was easier to fill a bucket off the viner.

I recall many fun times on the farm with friends and their families, including new American friends from the Weedons McMurdo base. It was the cocktail crazy 1950s and they would arrive with crushed-ice machines and barbeque steaks the size of plates. We indulged them by shucking and serving fresh Bluff oysters by the sack or flipping hearty patties loaded with West Coast whitebait. The Irish parish priest was a regular attendee. He loved to show his dab hand on the pool table and discuss the prospects of the trotters at Addington with Father, who had a penchant for the square gaiter. We went to many local country race meetings and an annual highlight was the A&P show, for which Mother sat up until 3am making the girls new dresses. We spent our "show pocket money" on dolls on sticks and candy floss.

I love a photo of the full family on a gate at the farm adjacent to the house. It brings back memories of the farm and the life we had there as a family. We were photographed there in 1969 and some of us more recently in 2006. The gate is still there, now surrounded by lifestyle blocks, while the original house has been modernised.

Paula Ryan (below, at right) and family at home.

Growing up on a farm in a large, close family provided the platform and stability for early personal growth. It grounded us and installed the qualities of resilience, strength and independence. As Kiwi kids, growing up in New Zealand, I don't think we appreciate our early years until we become parents and grandparents, and then reflect on what our own parents provided and the sacrifices they made.

Paula Ryan, MNZM, is a fashion personality and household name in New Zealand who embraces every project with positive enthusiasm. She was the founder of Fashion Quarterly and Simply You publishing companies. Both publishing companies she sold: Fashion Quarterly in 1990 to Australian Consolidated Press, the Simply You stable of three publications to A.P.N. Apart from being a recognised entrepreneur in publishing, Paula Ryan has developed a brand around her own name, developing a scientifically focused collection of clothing. This collection now sells in more than 150 stores; 105 in Australia, 45 in New Zealand. The Paula Ryan brand is also licensed to several companies who have developed complementary merchandise of pharmacy and fashion distribution. Apart from her own businesses she has been involved in external projects such as the design committee for the Commonwealth Games, international consultant to Merino New Zealand and style consultant to various airlines at various times.

Rāpaki: a place of quiet revolution.

Jane Bowron

Rāpaki

Every time I go down to Rāpaki I have the overwhelming urge to break into a sudden burst of applause.

I didn't cotton on to this nesting place till about 10 years ago when I returned home to the South to live in Christchurch for a seven-year stint.

The first time I rolled down the hill in the car, to discover that Rāpaki was more than just a beach — well two, actually — I kicked myself for not having followed previous instincts to swerve left at its signpost located midway from the port of Lyttelton on the way to Governors Bay.

How I regret those wasted afternoons vying for laid-out towel space back around the corner at Corsair Bay, the preferred bathing option of Tribe Bogan who like to drink beers there and swig up large before hurling themselves into the brine to cavort clumsily in sodden jeans.

Unless you got up very early in the morning in the summer holidays, a swim at Corsair Bay meant you had to deal with herds of inky-fleshed bodies overly embroidered with death cult tattoos, and the shriek of their foul-mouthed epithets echoing loudly round the beach's natural amphitheatre.

For anyone who knows me,

that last somewhat prissy statement is rich, coming from a person who swears like a drunken sailor. Old journalists' habits die hard and I remember having to make a conscious effort to watch my language when I returned to blend in to the niceties of Christchurch.

And it didn't do me any harm. I enjoy swearing but I realise from years of television reviewing and watching American and British programmes where the dialogue is often a flow of repeated expletives strung together with a bit of action thrown in, continued cuss words murder the vocabulary.

I mention this because it's pertinent to my experience of visiting Rāpaki and the effect of that beach where words seem redundant and the aesthetic is one of peace, bro'. Having found meditation impossible, and its fashionable offshoot "mindfulness" a bridge too far for this rough beast, the art of "being clear and present in the moment" at this beach is for me, in the words of Jack Nicholson, about "as good as it gets".

> **'When I was a kid, I wanted the drama of the surf to pit myself against to catch a free ride on a wave, but now as a mature bather, paddler and general wanderer of beaches, I look for a calm sea.'**

Rāpaki is more than a beach, there are many parts to it and bathing isn't its only attraction. It has a small village settled by the Ngāti Wheke tribe who suffered at the hands of Te Rauparaha, the great warrior chief attacking the settlement in 1831 and in his haste, leaving behind his pūtōrino flute, found later and donated to the Auckland Museum.

There is also a recently restored marae complex, a good jetty, and a small picturesque Catholic church. First opened in 1874, the church has a well-maintained fenced-off bone yard, which you can walk past and peruse the grave stones before getting to the goat track path that takes you down to the beaches.

In high tide there is the main beach and a smaller beach you can access from a short flight of stone steps built into the rocks. At low tide you can walk to the smaller more boulderish beach round a point, or swim to it safely from the longer sandy beach.

The path is too narrow for a wheelchair and has slight inclines, till the short walk takes you to a sloping grass area, ideal for picnics and a temporary day-at-the-beach campsite for those who prefer spreading out the rug and towels on grass, rather than the crumb-in-bottom togs grit incurred from perching in the sand.

During the big quake of 22 February 2011 a huge boulder broke off from the Port Hills, which towers over Rāpaki, and gathering a terrifying momentum, took out a house below in the village. For weeks photographs of that house and its ruin appeared in newspapers as an enduring image of the power of the destruction on that awful day.

On the up side, the aftershocks located around Banks Peninsula since the 7.1 quake have resulted in renewed hot springs activity. Small manmade pools have been dug out to allow basking in the tepid thermal temperatures. I remember being astounded to see the spectacle of the two white swans, regular habitués who hung out at the beach, make a bee-line for the warm spots.

As a Pākehā who suspects that a great grandmother on my mother's side may have been Māori from around Akaroa in Banks Peninsula, I have sometimes felt self-conscious and uneasy about being something of an intruder in Rāpaki, but the locals have never questioned my credentials or presence there.

When I was a kid, I wanted the drama of the surf to pit myself against to catch a free ride on a wave, but now as a mature bather, paddler and general wanderer of beaches, I look for a calm sea.

Overlooking Quail Island, Rāpaki beach is a tranquil place for someone like me who most often swims alone, and at this benign spot doesn't have to worry about dangerous rips or block-knocking *"Donald where's your trousers?"* thunderous surf.

Much has been written about the restorative powers of salt water and its happy mood-enhancing effects, which can be procured from any unpolluted New Zealand beach. Rāpaki has another level of mood enhancement because it takes me to a pre-conceptual state that shuts up the endless chatter of the inner monologue and provides a break from the dull demands of cold hard boring technology.

Who wants to stare at a computer screen or be an eye slave to the — me, myself and I-Phone that puts the blinkers on the bigger picture? Rāpaki reminds of a beautiful watercolour painting that you can wander into and enter to become part of the artist's scenery. I accept that even that romantic idea is an artificial construct harking back to an older screen of the painter's frame, but it is a far gentler one.

The only other place that has had a similar effect on me is the tiny west Hebrides island of Iona where I could feel a battle play out between the pagan and the Christian on a piece of land three miles long and a mile wide.

The spirituality present in Rāpaki is nameless, not wishy-washily secular but a place of quiet revolution against the machine. Once when I had swum out a-ways from the beach I turned to look back and see a helicopter landing on the slope of the grass, completely flattening the surrounding vegetation. Someone had broken their leg badly and had to be choppered out of there. I remember being initially curious and concerned for the victim, but felt a shameful resentment at the necessary evil intrusion of the helicopter on "my" unspoiled landscape.

They say possession is nine-tenths of the law and at the risk of sounding like an old hippie, I know that the land and the sea is un-ownable, that only a control freak seeks ultimate possession of it and we are all just visitors to the shore. All that can be owned is a response to a particular place, and that shadowy feeling — could we have been here some time before?

Jane Bowron is a freelance journalist based in Wellington. She is currently a television critic and general columnist for Fairfax newspapers and has been a feature writer, agony aunt columnist, and a media commentator. Her book of poems, Scenes Away from the Crime *was published in 1984 with the help of a Creative New Zealand Grant. In 2011 she wrote of her first-hand experiences of the Christchurch earthquake, with her regular dispatches from the Red Zone appearing in* The Press *and the* Dominion Post. *Her book* Old Bucky & Me *about her account of living through the quakes was published by AWA Press and was recommended by* The Lonely Planet Guide.

Jane Bowron gets as close to mindfulness as she can.

Waitaki River Valley: where the river surges blue in spring spate.

Fiona Farrell

Waitaki River Valley

Most of the time I move about the surface of the earth without paying much attention to my surroundings. I sit here at my desk and outside, neatly framed by the window, there's a landscape: bucolic, sheep, the neighbour's orange grader parked under some bluegums, hills, bushclad. There's a sound-track: baa baa, tweet tweet, the rhythmic breathing of the sea in counterpoint to the tapping of my keyboard. And there are smells: sea weed and sea salt, honeysuckle and sheep pooh.

When I first arrived here 20 or so years ago, I noticed this landscape, in the same way that I notice the detail of a new house. For a brief period when I move in, it matters where I place things I like or use. I notice the fall of light and arrange chairs and beds just so. I shelve the books, hang the paintings I've carried about with me from one place to another, being very particular: not too high, not too low, nail holes peppering the Gib as I try to get it right. And then I stop. And everything stays pretty much where it was first placed until some irresistible event — a new job, major renovation, quake or fire or divorce — forces change.

Newness, unfamiliarity, is one reason a landscape lodges in the memory.

Such landscapes are glimpses, not necessarily of major destinations, not grand or compelling or, God help us, "iconic". More often, they are unremarkable. A stretch of tree-lined road, a flat-topped hill glimpsed at sunset, a grubby city street. But for some reason, they have imprinted, to return to the inward eye at unexpected intervals, as I am driving to the supermarket or doing the dishes or falling to sleep. Novelty has lent them clarity, that same clarity you sense in the work of travel writers who skim into a city or a country for a day or two, opinions quickly formed, characters delineated before they can become complex creatures of contrary moods and experience, landscapes observed with all the hypnotic intensity of jet lag, dislocation and an unfamiliar bed.

The random return of such landscapes is usually a pleasurable sensation. It's as though I possess a surprising little inner gallery, which is apt, given that the term I've just discovered, by looking up my beautiful ancient *Shorter Oxford Dictionary* — was an artist's word. Those prolific Dutch artists of the seventeenth century invented it to differentiate their work from "seascapes". "Landscapes" were inland images, of calm cows and windmills rather than the restless imagery of boats hove to in a raging sea, bearing spices and good things back to the happy burghers of Amsterdam and Delft. The background to saints and seated Virgins bearing the plump haloed baby had quietly moved to the foreground, shedding religion on the way.

> There's a soundtrack: baa baa, tweet tweet, the rhythmic breathing of the sea in counterpoint to the tapping of my keyboard. And there are smells: sea weed and sea salt, honeysuckle and sheep pooh.

I like that. It does indeed feel as if those glimpsed landscapes of mine occupy the memory gallery with a simple, satisfying inland calm.

Others however are more complicated.

Years ago, I spent more time than was strictly useful studying T. S. Eliot. He was big and heavy and once he swapped interesting youthful neurosis for High Anglican certainty, really a bit of a bore. But some things he wrote have stayed with me. One in particular was his notion of the "objective correlative". He observed that a writer creating a fictional world for the stage or in a novel, has to select "a set of objects, a situation, a chain of events which shall be the formula" of the emotion he or she is seeking to arouse in a reader or theatre audience.

We all create narratives of our lives, and the landscapes that are the setting for this tale are not neutral. They are full of feeling, some good, some bad. Some of the landscapes in my interior gallery are anything but sunwashed. They are not happy little daubs that will match the curtains. They are dark, or painful, or mouldy with regret. They also arise at unexpected moments, and it is best, then, not to stay too long. Better to walk away.

I am 68 this year. Recently, I've noticed a new kind of conversation. It's the one where I find myself talking with friends about where we want to be buried, or flung to the four winds as flakes of ash. We talk about it in the way we would once have talked about whether or not we should move overseas or to another suburb or out to the country on account of the fresh vegetables and the children and the dog. What landscape should we choose for our final purpose? It is I suppose, the definitive "landscape of the heart" not to mention the liver, kidneys and all the other bits of which we are so temporarily composed.

I'm not sure what I'd choose: should it be a landscape of childhood? That intricately observed world where the Jersey Bennes formed lush rows and the concrete by the back door split over a meandering crack opening to the underworld and rows of marching ants, every detail judged of equal beauty and astonishment, from the scarlet drop of red currants to the stink of a dead hedgehog, seething metropolis of white millions. Or the wider landscape beyond the front gate into which we moved, step by step, until we had walked all the way to the corner, where eventually we turned and walked away altogether? That glistening Eden that entrances in the dullest autobiography, before it all dwindles to maturity and the tedious recital of things achieved, places visited, and the plop plop plop of names dropping.

Or should my heart be tucked into one of the loved landscapes of adult life? The broad sweep of the Waitaki Valley where the river still surges creamy blue in spring spate, unlike its sad sisters to the north, drained to the dusty nubbin. Or Dansey's Pass with its brown quilt of tussock tossing this way then that in a stiff wind? Or a city street? Should I be poured into a drain on George Street or Carlton Mill Road on a winter night, lights reflecting in icy puddles? Or a beach, any beach, on these perfect islands, east coast or west, Pacific blue or Tasman black, tangled with flayed timber or bulky with boulders or smoothed for the evening stroll. Or this little bay perhaps with its irritable oyster catchers and lava cliffs where the voices of seals echo in deep caverns?

Any one of them would do.

Since her first novel received the New Zealand Fiction Award in 1992, Fiona Farrell has published novels, short fiction, poetry and non-fiction. Her most recent work, The Villa at the Edge of the Empire, *is a study of the Christchurch earthquakes. In 2007, she received the Prime Minister's Award for Fiction, and in 2012, the ONZM for Services to Literature. Born in Ōamaru, she now lives and works in the dramatic landscape of Otanerito on Banks Peninsula.*

Fiona's cousin Patrick holding the cricket bat, sister Moira and Fiona, with her father in the doorway of the Power Board crib.

Patrick, Moira, Fiona's mother and Fiona by the little red Austen Standard.

Somewhere north of Haast: the place found by accident.

Brando Yelavich

Somewhere on the West Coast

I don't know what my landscape is called or whether it has a name that anyone would know. I came across it when I was doing my walk around New Zealand's coastline, so it was just one part of the coast as far as I was concerned.

It was so wild and different from anything else I'd ever seen. It was totally untouched and had obviously been let loose to go wild for a very long time — possibly forever. I felt like I had finally reached the middle of nowhere.

It was about 300 days into my journey. Walking the West Coast in winter is probably the most miserable thing you can put yourself through. It's wet, it's cold, it never stops raining and there are sandflies even in winter.

But this spot stood out as a place that was incredibly beautiful, even after all the other beautiful places I had seen. I don't know how to describe how beautiful it was. It was a bit like walking onto the set of a movie that's had so many special effects thrown at it it's not funny.

The closer you get to the coast in that part of the country, the thicker the bush gets. The brush is sharp and not at all friendly. It was so thick and the foliage was so tough that I was moving only about two or three kilometres a day.

Getting there was mentally as well as physically demanding.

There wasn't even a track to it. I had been bush bashing for three or four days when I came across it. It was a stormy day and I had had to cross a river which was extra high as the result of a storm.

I had gone in with a bit of local knowledge. Someone told me I could get around the bottom of the cliffs from the beach. But when I was there the swell was massive and kept smashing me against the cliffs. I got stuck there for eight or nine hours because of the tides.

> ❛I didn't stay in any one part for more than a day. Although it was absolutely beautiful, it wasn't somewhere I wanted to linger because of how miserable and wet it was.❜

To get into the bush itself was incredibly difficult. I had to climb a limestone cliff to get up from the beach. And once on top the terrain went up and down, up and down. I don't know where I was. I felt like I'd been walking forever and was never going to get anywhere.

But eventually I came out on top of another cliff and there was this beautiful long stretch of beach with nothing on it apart from a few deer walking majestically along. I must have scared them because they made a noise — it was the first time I'd heard a deer make any kind of sound and I got freaked out.

Because the place was so untouched there was a massive amount of birdlife running riot — tūī, wood pigeons, lots of seagulls.

On the first night, I had to clear away supplejack before I could set up my tent. I settled down, but all through the night I could hear raucous birds. When I woke up in the morning my campsite was surrounded by Fiordland crested penguins, standing there staring at me. It's quite likely they had never seen a human before.

It took four days to walk through the whole area. I didn't stay in any one part for more than a day. Although it was absolutely beautiful, it wasn't somewhere I wanted to linger because of how miserable and wet it was.

The part of the cliff I came upon when I got through the bush was obviously a very exposed part of the cliff line because on the top there were deep pools surrounded by lush green foliage. It was like walking out on a perfectly mown patch of grass with pools dotted around it. And there were waterfalls cascading down into each one. I had a bath in one overlooking the view of the beach.

Anyone thinking of going there should definitely tell someone before they leave. Every few steps there's some form of danger in your path. There are massive drops and every 100 metres or so there would be a gorge — a narrow crack in the ground in the middle of the bush where water had worn it away over thousands of years and created a three or four metre pool with limestone at the top.

I found my way mainly by following animal tracks. Normally if you go 200 or so metres in from the coast you'll find deer or goat tracks. That's where they walk because it's safer. You need to follow those tracks because it's very easy to get lost when you can't hear the sea any more.

Everything was just that much harder because I had too much equipment when I set off, a lot of which I didn't need. But there was also a lot of heavy safety gear weighing me down. I had a spot tracker which transmitted my location every 10 minutes regardless of what I was doing. I also had a satellite phone.

The Wildboy adventure has changed my life. Originally I did it in order to escape from a lot of crappy stuff that was happening, but so much has come out of it that I could never have predicted and it's given me the lifestyle I've always wanted.

Now I take people on my adventures. I would think about taking them to this space. It's practical. But I always let people know that if they're coming with me it will probably be the most adventurous thing they've done in their lives. They'll be travelling with one of the most adventurous people in New Zealand so will be 100 per cent outside their comfort zone.

But this is what a lot of people are looking for. They want to push themselves, but they want to be with someone who knows what they're doing.

Because I don't charge people to come with me I don't have to keep to some of the safety regulations that commercial tours do, so it's a real adventure. I think that's what people need — to deal with real risks and face the consequences.

There's nothing wrong with falling down a bank and cutting your leg open.

Now I'm doing a diploma in adventure tourism, not so much because I'm interested in tourism but because it will teach me how to give people experiences in a reasonably safe way.

Whether anyone wants to come with me or not, I'm determined to go back to that place one day.

Brando Yelavich walked around the entire coast of New Zealand in 2013-14, a journey recorded in his book Wildboy. *He now runs Wildboy Adventures which gives others the opportunity to develop their adventurous side.*

Brando Yelavich exploring the coast.

Geraldine: too sedentary for some.

Murray Crane

Geraldine

It's been more than 30 years since I packed my bag and reversed out of a familiar driveway in a hand-me-down car, leaving the small town that I still regard as home.

At the time, as a 17-year-old boy, I couldn't wait to say goodbye to the wide streets and narrow minds. The strict teachers, grumpy neighbours and over-familiar scoutmasters had taken their toll. Bright lights and the big smoke beckoned. This sedentary little town was no place for me.

Time has passed and I now fondly remember Geraldine for the idyllic childhood it allowed me to have. If New Zealand was 10 years behind the rest of the world in the 1970s, then this town, my town, was 20. It had a naivety and innocence about it that I mistook for ignorance and tranquillity as boredom.

We once went on an eight-week holiday and didn't lock our doors. The lawns were mown when we returned. Milk money was left out, the movies were paid for with a coin (sometimes the same one) and cigarettes were as bad as it got.

We read *Commando* comics and visited the local RSA where elderly men whispered about their actual wartime exploits.

> **'Hay bales scattered the landscape, their golden hue refracted by sunsets still checked by shepherds who rode horses like cowboys and drank beer from brown bottles.'**

Hay bales scattered the landscape, their golden hue refracted by sunsets still checked by shepherds who rode horses like cowboys and drank beer from brown bottles. School galas were our crowd funding and pocket money was in short supply. We had nowhere to spend it anyway and made our own fun on homemade bikes and carts down hills and through riverbeds — no helmets, sunscreen, cellphones or bike locks.

Home by dark.

South Island summer days were long and hot, we swam in rivers and stole grapes and apples off neighbours' trees. Fish and chips on a Friday night.

We stared at Asian tourists who stopped to pee and shot things (and each other) with air rifles.

In winter we went to woolshed parties, warmed by bonfires and smuggled spirits.

By age 15 cars were our freedom, sanctuary and our escape. I lost my innocence in the back of one and drove too fast on shingle roads where we loved, laughed and died. The blood we spilled ebbs through me now; ordinary yet unfamiliar.

Murray Crane bases himself in Auckland where he runs his eponymous label Crane Brothers. Tailoring suits for the rich and famous is a long way from school holidays spent working on farms nestled at the foothills of the Southern Alps. The South Island will always be home for this sixth-generation mainlander.

Murray Crane when Geraldine was just the right size.

Nor'-west arch over freshly ploughed land, near Geraldine.

Te Moana Waterfall: pummelling and cleansing.

Jordan Luck

Te Moana River Waterfall

I drive up the valley, up the gorge. I follow the millowing, willowing winding Te Moana River. Sunshine beats down on the roof of my parents' Volkswagen Kombi. I hear shingle being scratched out of the grave gravelled grooves in the oven rutted road. I watch dust, powder into the air, caking the trees and the green baking leaves along the swerving curving roadside. Windows down. A tear of happiness carves a river through the dust that clings to my face. We listen to a Sunday request show on Radio Caroline. The Bass and The Tweeters go to war as Alice Cooper considers Richard Nixon, contemplates presidential election and croons "School's Out". "My, what a wonderful voice she has," says the D.J. There are four of us and we are heading to The Waterfall.

Labor Omnia Vincit. Work Conquers All. It is our school motto. It is very appropriate. I'm not 18, I am 15. I am a haycarter. I make a lot of money. I will never make more money per minute until 2013. I do not need to buy a Golden Kiwi. The haycarting crew, three, four, five of us, take our girlfriends/boyfriends to flash restaurants in Timaru and buy Filet Mignon and Harvey Wallbangers.

I am not into the money, I am into The Work. Sol Lucet Omnibus. The sun shines over everyone. I hope so. Definitely hay. Make hay while the sun shines. This too is appropriate. Idiom, proverb? It is *the* truth. We have borne the brunt of those who have crucified us in doing otherwise. Grass has been cut and in the hot South Canterbury sun it dries. A machine, a hay baler arrives. It turns rows and rows of grass into haybales, rectangular haybales, about a metre long, half metre high, half metre wide. Grass converted into a ladylike, manhandable shape. Weight of very very variable. You would lose dosh trying to estimate. The bale, bound by two strands of twine, leather gloved, you attack. The bonds in grasp, you snatch and snab and clean and jerk and work the dried fodder upwards and away. Not a skerrick of a second can be delayed. The truck is moving. Leather chaps. Leather chaps, they protect *everything* below the waist.

If the bale is well-dried grass, near crispy, you can throw these beasts six tiers high to get to your seventh. Mmmn, with a low-based deck truck you can throw eight. Nine on an illustrious day. You take these stacked trucks to a haybarn and restack. I love driving by the old barns we stacked. We were and are lucky haycarters. Round bales (and super super rectangles) became The Vogue, The Word, the front cover of *Country Life* and put paid to the industry. ″Rrrrround bale the landscape, why don'tcha″. A romp, a roll, a tup in the . . . is never gonna be the same. Labor Omnia Vincit 'til there is none.

> **❝A tear of happiness carves a river through the dust that clings to my face. We listen to a Sunday request show on Radio Caroline.❞**

It bucketed and poured, it bucketed and poured, the sky near impaled us with its treacherous roar. Fields amok, from fence to fence. A 13-, 14-, 15-minute, 16-minute drench. It is only just past 11.

Norwegian pop band of "Take On Me" renown. Blue sky. Bluest blue sky. No more baling today. No more Precious McKenzie, no more Graham May hayhem. What more can a poor boy do with a Kombi and an afternoon off? ″Well, that's it″, "Bugger," said Mr Nugent in a Fred Dagg kinda voice. "Mr Nugent, is it okay to borrow your phone?" I enquired. "Yep, Moira. Lunch. Up there. Up there anyway. Thanks. Tomorrow. Tomorrow morning?" Stuart and Andrew have other escapades so I have already decided to call Bill. "Thank you, Mrs Nugent. Love the silverside." Ramble yarn ramble rained out. "You know, you know Stephanie ay?" sez Bill. "Mmmm huh . . . yeah," I remotely hazard. "Well . . . Steph's coming here. Josephine too. Waterfall?"

Montgomery. I said I loved The Work. Yes, true. However, there are two things that kinda make it easy to differentiate between "I Love Haycarting" and "I Love You, Haycarting". One is thistles. I look at a paddock and I sometimes say to myself "I think I might just go Grubbing this afternoon". This can be a beggar when you travel a lot and don't have a grubber.

Thistle is but a prick. Montgomery? Montgomery Red is a clover. This wee beasty has a dust that will bury, itch, weasel its way into your pores. A shower will not suffice. I am unthistled but am covered in thousands of billions of unluminous Montgomery Spheres. Caked.

The Te Moana Waterfall is pummelling. The deluge a few hours ago is commanding. I will soon be cleansed. It is 30 metres of powerful shower with a cave at the back. You have to yell to hear one another. You have to near scream to hear one another. You can whisper. Josephine and I whisper. We dive 30 metres, we swim, we dive, we dive, we swim. We whisper.

It is 24 years and many moons later. I listen to Buffy Saint Marie's "Little Wheel, Spin & Spin" as I drive up the valley, up the gorge. I follow the millowing, willowing winding Te Moana River. I clamber to the top of Te Moana River Waterfall. I throw my father's ashes. I dive.

Jordan Luck is best known as front person of The Exponents (previously Dance Exponents) and for such crowd-pleasing classics as "Why Does Love Do This to Me?" and "Victoria". In a more than 35-year career he has won numerous awards including being named the first inductee into the New Zealand Music Hall of Fame. In 2012 he was named a member of the New Zealand Order of Merit for services to music. In 2015 The Exponents received the Legacy Award at the New Zealand Music Awards.

Jordan Luck between dives.

Jo Seagar

High Country

When I was a child, I loved pioneering farming stories — New Zealand stories of real life and real people. Georg Kohlap's iconic *David, Boy of the High Country* and a book called *Katie One Summer*. The Joyce West novels — *Drover's Road*, *The Golden Country* and *Cape Lost*. I worked my way through *Lady Barker's Diaries* and Mona Anderson's *A River Rules My Life* and insidiously, without my being fully aware anything was happening, that sneaky High Country consciousness slowly slipped into my psyche.

I experienced the strange emotional pull of the hills. It is an extraordinary connection and felt by many Kiwi. It seems to be part of our DNA.

It wasn't until I was a young teenager, about 13 I think, that I first visited any part of New Zealand that could remotely — excuse the pun — be called the High Country. A kind of unofficially mapped area of dry eastern tussock grassland landscapes in the rain shadow between the coastal plains and the main mountain divide in the South Island.

I had been invited down South to go skiing with Canterbury cousins for the old-style August school holidays.

The road up over Porter's Pass was built in 1865 — named for the

High Country: where the sheds put the landscape in context.

local Porter brothers, who farmed big runs in the area at that time. It was a winding, rutted bullock wagon track, but importantly, connected Canterbury and its early settlers to the gold fields of the West Coast.

It was 90 years later that I was born — 1955. A tiny five-pound scrap of a baby, who survived and thrived thanks to glorious Mother Nature and the post-natal care of Saint George's Hospital, Christchurch. That block is now lost to the earthquakes of 2010 and 2011. So I was born on the mainland, but my childhood home was Hawke's Bay.

We often visited grandparents and family in Christchurch, and this particular holiday was to ski at Broken River. The road to the summit of Porter's Pass is the steep bit of the journey. A winding gravelly and slow climb. I clearly remember Holga's old Volvo station wagon struggling somewhat with the big load aboard and him pulling over in the layby (affectionately known in our family as a "restarea") at the top to stretch our legs. I think this was 1960s code for a badly needed cigarette or two and a rest from a car full of teenage girls threatening vomiting at every hairpin bend.

> **The view from the top of Porter's is amazing. Behind us the green patchwork plains and outwash of stony braided riverbeds of Canterbury. Up ahead, the glorious vast tussock billowing grasslands and rocky outcrops. The huge emptiness. The beech forests. The tan coloured sweep of the hills. And the shimmering grey streaks of the scree.**

The view from the top of Porter's is amazing. Behind us the green patchwork plains and outwash of stony braided riverbeds of Canterbury. Up ahead, the glorious vast tussock billowing grasslands and rocky outcrops. The huge emptiness. The beech forests. The tan coloured sweep of the hills. And the shimmering grey streaks of the scree.

I will never forget my first sight of this place and the unexplained felling of coming home. Of the rightness at being in "my" high country. Perhaps I'd had a previous life here or probably just been a very imaginative child, but it felt familiar.

I am a sixth-generation Kiwi and from early Canterbury settler gene lines, so perhaps it is in my blood. My mother had told us stories of riding her bike over Porter's as a Rangi Ruru school girl in the 1930s. She pointed out a roadman's hut that they had camped in — it is still there. Her father and uncles were the infamous Matson brothers, stock and station agents. They were probably the ones selling the horses, gold pans and shovels to the newly landed immigrants heading to the gold rush on the Coast.

I'd grown up on stories of their escapades, and I knew they were most famous for always getting the supplies though — namely the grog!

I was a farm girl. I could drive a tractor — an old David Brown — when I was eight. As children we had helped with mustering on horseback and feeding out. I'd been a roustabout in the wool shed during the shearing and done my fair portion of lambing beats and arm-breaking haymaking. So the outdoorsy

aspect of the High Country was not completely unknown to me. But that was a tame farming childhood in Havelock North compared to this wild craggy place.

I loved that first ski trip to Broken River, even with its real hardships compared to today's skiing holidays. We had to trek up from the carpark, through the beech forest and out above it to the snowline and the ski clubhouse, carrying our backpacks and skis over our shoulders. My buddy Karen and I were too cool for words. We skied in Granny's fur jackets and jeans — my brother's Wranglers. No bibbed ski suit in bri-nylon for us. It was homespun jerseys, woollen mittens, pompom hats and oilskins.

Skis were so long and made of varnished wood, with cable bindings and lace-up boots. Our heavy packs were full of essentials — Fanta and Pinky bars, Minties and records. We couldn't go a week without *Easy Rider*, the Carpenters and David Bowie. We carried huge, probably glass, bottles of shampoo and conditioner for our long Carly Simon hair and a big load of Q-Tol and Chapstick for the inevitable sunburnt face. I remember the panda look with goggle tans.

I returned often and have skied all the different club fields in the area — Temple Basin, Craigieburn, Olympus, Cheeseman and Porter Heights.

The Seagar move to Oxford in North Canterbury 10 years ago wasn't just a fluke, put-a-pin-on-the-map-and-let's-go-there decision. No, the close proximity to my favourite mountains and the high country and Porter's Pass was a big deciding factor. Oxford is also on scenic Route 73.

My great friend Chrissie Fernyhough owned Castle Hill Station. Many of you will have read her wonderful books *The Road to Castle Hill* and *Ben & Mark*. Chrissie had also relocated out of Auckland, and at about the same time as us.

Those who know Chrissie well are aware of her legendary hospitality and kindness in sharing Castle Hill with friends and visitors. We spent wonderful times up there, and I have precious memories of long hot days, picnics up on the bluffs, gin & tonics on the rocks — literally the rocky outcrops that give Castle Hill its name.

We have camped way out the back at the River Hut or in the now luxurious Old Quarters, the Limestone Cottage or the Roadman's Hut. Nights of stargazing — such big skies — counting satellites, sorting out the problems of the world, laughing, singing, telling yarns.

I learnt to drive a digger at Castle Hill — a handy skill! And to drink single malt whisky — perhaps not so handy.

After my childhood ski clubbing years and visits to this area, I returned a number of times during my nursing years when I had learnt to fly. My planes of choice were old tail draggers — real planes. Tiger Moths, Piper Cubs and Cessna 180s. I loved the feeling of flying in the hills. Learning to read the weather and conditions. Swooping down the valleys. Dodging downdrafts and flying through the Torlesse Gap. Dad had told me that it was a badge of experience and skill when he was in the Air Force if you took your plane through the Gap — you could claim you were a real flyboy.

I am a real flyboy!

Ross and I have also been very fortunate to enjoy the friendship of the Stephenson family, who owned Saint James Station up near Molesworth. We have had the privilege of experiencing this other particular wild and beautiful part of New Zealand's High Country — up the Ada.

We have helped with cattle musters and attended the wild horse sales. Fished in the tarns and mountain lakes. Helped with weed control, removing broom and wilding pines, as we travelled around the station. The Seagar children both learnt to drive way out in this remote area, including how to ford rivers.

I loved our family holidays up there and our children speak of these trips as the best of times. The best holidays, even compared with Disneyland. I loved cooking on the old wood-fired range. We all spent hours cutting firewood and kindling to keep the old gal going. I channelled those tough pioneering women who had been there before me. How hard was that life with such rare contact with the outside world. Delivering your own babies and burying a few too. No radio or phone or internet. The constant mending, preparing food, preserving, cooking, cleaning, washing and trying to get it all dry. No microfiber, Gortex or polyfleece in those days. Wet wool and thick cotton. No days off or minimum wage. The work was never ending for these women — if the men were well fed, the farm was well run.

Both of my children learnt how to make a good proper roast from scratch in the high country — killing the sheep, preparing it, peeling spuds and pumpkin, filling the firebox and making traditional gravy — no meal has tasted so good.

I can almost smell the memory — wild mountain thyme herbaceous salty tasting Merino mutton, thick nourishing gravy, crispy (read charred) roast vegetables, smoky tasting apple pie and warm thick cream.

How lucky I am that by some extraordinary roll of the dice or flip of the coin my ancestors got on ships out of the depressed, unemployed, hopeless United Kingdom and potato famine Ireland and somehow got to God's Own Country. I feel it every time I drive up that Porter's Pass road — now a smooth sealed highway.

The rising sun paints the bluffs golden autumnal natural colours. The tussock sways in the howling nor'-wester. It is hot and dry, but often with snow on the tops. The vast emptiness. The constantly changing landscape. The challenge of it all. Not many bars of cellphone coverage up here! No-one about.

I lift mine eyes to the hills and I am connected. I am tangata whenua in this place.

Jo was born in Christchurch and grew up in rural Hawke's Bay. Her father, Martyn, was a farmer and her mother, Fay, was a practising lawyer. Having a working mother, especially involved in the legal profession, was very unusual in the fifties and sixties, and a capable father who drove the children to all school events and was an excellent cook was also different for the times. While living in London Jo attended the Cordon Bleu cookery school and La Varenne culinary school in Paris. In the late 1990s Jo became a well-known face in New Zealand living rooms with her television cooking show on TV One, the highest rated primetime show on TVNZ at the time. Jo now writes a column for the Australian Women's Weekly. *Children Kate and Guy live close by and Jo has two grandsons and is enjoying teaching them the joys of cooking.*

Jo Seagar reaches for the sky.

MacKenzie Country: even the getting there is magical.

Jodi Brown

MacKenzie Country

Life as a semi professional netballer has taken me all around New Zealand, and I have been lucky enough to experience many parts of our beautiful country. Apart from Wanganui, where I grew up and lived until I was 16 and moved away to play netball, Dunedin is where I have spent the longest.

Lake Ruataniwha camping ground in Twizel has been my husband's and my summer camping holiday destination for the past 10 years and automatically became my favourite spot in New Zealand. Planning our camping trip, packing up the cars, boats, trailers and caravans and the anticipation of the road trip is so exciting that we start planning next year's trip the moment we leave.

Most people in this part of the world migrate towards Wānaka and Queenstown for their holidays, leaving only a few of us to enjoy this beautiful spot.

Even the three-hour journey from Dunedin is magical, as we leave the city and head into the country. There's the annual stop in

Kurow for an ice cream and a play at the park (since we had kids). The view of lake after lake and the mountain ranges is simply spectacular.

On the long straight from Ōmarama to Twizel the excitement builds as we pass paddock after paddock of grass, often with irrigation systems at work, before reaching the salmon farm.

From that point we are officially in our "happy place" for the next three or four weeks. For our first few years here we camped in a small group which was mostly family. This has expanded into a great group of about seven families who we camp with.

We are blessed with access to wonderful places and scenery around the MacKenzie Country. We can choose between three lakes to swim and do water sports in and walk or bike around. On our door step we have Lake Ruataniwha, the smallest of the lakes and probably the busiest, being used for all sorts of activities — not just rowing competitions and racing but also a lot of water sports with boats and jet skis. There is also a calm lagoon where people can swim, kayak and play freely without competition from big powerboats.

> When telling people about our summer destination I really can't do it justice. The mix of the bright natural colours; the clean fresh air that makes you feel alive; the cold nights and foggy mornings that turn into scorching hot days; the freedom our kids get to experience in the outdoors, new friends and happy places and the memories that we all make . . .

I love how the lakes look so inviting each day and am often mesmerised by their colour — bright, bright, blue. It's mostly calm, although some days the wind arrives to muck up our plans. Being on the border of Central Otago we often experience high temperatures that send everyone into the water to cool off.

Just down the road, going south you have Lake Ōhau with Lake Benmore to the east — both bigger than Lake Ruataniwha. Lake Ōhau is the coldest and Lake Benmore the warmest. But both are very popular for boating activities and often you need to use a boat to find a quiet private spot to enjoy yourself.

Of course, if you want a change from the lakes there are scenic walks and on a clear sunny day there is nothing more spectacular than seeing Mount Cook rising high above everything else with its snow glowing in the distance. There are wonderful and various mountain tracks suitable for all levels, small ponds for fishing, a river which is often sheltered from the wind and safe for children to swim in and a beautiful township.

When telling people about our summer destination I really can't do it justice. The mix of the bright natural colours; the clean fresh air that makes you feel alive; the cold nights and foggy mornings that turn into scorching hot days; the freedom our kids get to experience in the outdoors, new friends and happy

places and the memories that we all make —
it's hard to contain them in two pages of a
book.

I fell in love with this part of New Zealand
from the moment I experienced it for the first
time and since then have never considered
being anywhere else for our summer holidays.

*Jodi Brown (née Te Huna; born 6 May 1981 in
Wanganui) is a retired netball player. Jodi was
a member of the Silver Ferns, from 2002 to 2015,
taking time off in between those periods due to
injury and pregnancy, earning 61 caps. She has also
played elite domestic netball for 13 years, her most
recent team being the Central Pulse in 2015 and was
getting set to play her final season in 2016 before
she injured her ACL and MCL in the preseason and
decided to retire from domestic netball after she had
retired from international netball in 2015.*

Jodi Brown has a choice of three lakes.

Mount Airini: you can see it all from here.

William Rolleston

Mount Airini

Late autumn, just before the first snowfall, is the best time to hike up Mount Airini in the hill country of coastal South Canterbury. The air is crisp and clear. The Pacific Ocean stretches to the horizon. Visible are the Ōamaru headland, the North Otago Coast and the Canterbury Bight curving to the Port Hills which looks like the island Captain Cook once thought it was. Beyond, Tapuaenuku and the other snow-capped mountains of the Kaikōura range poke above the horizon some 250 miles away.

So much local farming and family history is below me. To the north-east, The Levels Station, where my great-great-grandfather, George Rhodes, brought the first sheep to South Canterbury and made his home in the 1850s.

It was from him that Scottish drover James McKenzie stole a thousand sheep in 1855 and took them to the hinterland. And it was at the MacKenzie Pass (later named for McKenzie), just north of here that the thief was captured by Taiko and Sidebottom and then escaped the same night.

The port of Timaru, its modern container cranes just visible across the city, was a key hub for settlement and early trade. In 1859 *The Strathallan* arrived from Gravesend with 100 British settlers on board. George Rhodes lodged the arrivals in his woolshed on the first night and offered them two weeks of employment.

Farmland stretches to the coast, taken up by settlers and returned servicemen after the breakup of the large farming estates and in recognition for a job well done.

The contribution to the land of the Ōpuha Dam is clear to see. Patches of green across otherwise brown paddocks remind me of the importance of water to the social, economic and environmental outcomes for South Canterbury. This area has been amongst the fastest growing regions since the dam was built in 1998.

A grey warbler flits on the wind in a vertical dance and, with his long trilled song, drops down again amongst the tussocks and rock as his voice fades. It seems such a fruitless way to find a mate in such a big landscape, but he is a survivor, unlike the great eagle, Te Pouākai, which once ruled this territory. Gone too are the moa it hunted.

Fingers of native bush cling to the steep and shady gullies, driven back by a drying climate and fire, set by ancient hunters, farmers and lightning. Tree stumps are reminders of the tōtara forest which stood on these slopes before the arrival of humans a millennium ago.

> **'A grey warbler flits on the wind in a vertical dance and, with his long trilled song, drops down again amongst the tussocks and rock as his voice fades. It seems such a fruitless way to find a mate in such a big landscape, but he is a survivor, unlike the great eagle.'**

Mount Airini is in the Hunters Hills — named by surveyor Charles Torlesse for its reputation as a good place for the local iwi to hunt food. Local chieftain Te Huruhuru, who told Torlesse about the bountiful hunting available in the hills, is remembered with his name given to one of the highest peaks.

Torlesse named the most prominent mountain, although not the tallest, Nimrod — the hunter from biblical times — and its prominence means it also has significance for local Maori.

Well before European settlement a travelling party, led by chief Te Kaumira, were caught in a snow storm while crossing the hills. The party was separated and when the storm subsided and the party regathered chief Te Kaumira was missing. His body was found in a rock shelter. The Maori name of the range, Te Tari a Te Kaumira (The Hunters Hills),and the mountain below which he died, Te Tahu a Te Kaumira (Mount Nimrod), are in his memory.

Mount Airini and the Hunters Hills divide the down country of coastal South Canterbury from the high country of the upper Hakataramea Valley and the MacKenzie Country beyond.

On the east slopes tussock is watered by easterly cloud and mist which hangs late in the summer afternoon.

On the drier west slopes, rock, scree and speargrass is more prominent, sympathetic to the high country landscape and fighting against the harsh effects of the dry nor'-west. Hakataramea — the dance of the speargrass, commemorates a dance where the performers wore bags made from the skins of the whēkau (Laughing Owl) and filled with the sweet-scented gum from the flower stalks of the taramea (speargrass).

This is the country that frames my landscape — an essential elemental touchstone of my life, so inevitably I focus on what it means today.

The fifth generation of my family are growing up on Blue Cliffs Station on the rolling downs some thousand metres below my vantage point on Mount Airini.

Blue Cliffs — our tūrangawaewae since 1879.

It is at Blue Cliffs that my grandmother, Airini Woodhouse, found the last Laughing Owl dead on the side of the road in 1914. It was thought extinct and none has been identified since.

It was from Blue Cliffs that my ancestors, shepherds and neighbours would ride in the early hours of the morning to begin the muster from the top of the hills just as dawn was breaking.

It was on these slopes below in 1949 where, exhausted after two days of rescuing stock and battling fire, grandmother Airini, on her knees, asked for help. Within a short period an incoming heavy fog quelled the fires which flickered and died.

It was on these slopes that my grandfather, Dr Philip Woodhouse, chairman of the South Canterbury Catchment Board, came to realise the importance of water management and erosion control.

The boundary of the Blue Cliffs hill block, The Weaner Run, is only some 3.5 kilometres south along the ridgeline from Mount Airini. Less than ten years before she died at the age of 92, my grandmother walked those 3.5 kilometres and back with my mother, brother and me. Compulsory on those trips were hot water for tea, bran biscuits and maps of all sorts to orientate us not just to the now, not just to the landscape but also to the past.

Mount Airini stands at 1373 metres. It was a late autumn day in 1989, just before the first snowfall, that we journeyed up the winding farm track to the top of Mount Airini — me running (I was a keen runner), brother John and sister Liza on horseback and my father by vehicle.

We had come to spread Airini's ashes on the mountain named after her — we had come to say goodbye.

We said a prayer, drank our tea, ate our bran biscuits and made our way back down the hill.

Dr William Rolleston is National President of Federated Farmers of New Zealand and Vice President of the World Famers Organisation. William and his brother John farm Blue Cliffs Station — a 5000-hectare sheep and beef property in South Canterbury — which has been in the family since 1879. They have diversified the station to include a biologicals and pharmaceutical manufacturing export business — South Pacific Sera Ltd. As well as his business interests William has held board and strategic advisory positions relating to agriculture, science and economic development. He is a keen skier, has a degree in medicine, and in 2009 was awarded the Distinguished Biotechnologist of the Year for services to the biotechnology industry.

Mt Airini: William, Marion, Rachel (2.5yrs), Julia (4 months).

Central: the scent of wild thyme and so much more.

Peter Montgomery

Central Otago

It was the smell that hooked me.

Wild thyme — that scent so special and unique to the hills of Central Otago, especially in the area between Alexandra and Wānaka.

The strong hypnotic smell is unique to New Zealand, and if you walk the hills of Central when wild thyme is in flower, your clothes or pets hold the smell for days.

But there is so much more to Central Otago than the smell of wild thyme.

From November to January every year the hills colour up with a deep mauve that looks like a red haze. The Big Sky feel of space and expanse changes moods several times a day as the shadows of the sun dance across the foothills and the mountains in the distance. At night the Milky Way becomes an explosion of stars that you can spend hours gazing at.

I was introduced to this special part of New Zealand by my parents. Long ago, just before I was 10, we set off from Dunedin for Queenstown for a summer holiday. On the way, near Gabriel's Gully, in Lawrence, we had the misfortune to break the windscreen on our car. As a result our plans had to be changed and we were advised to go to Cromwell to await a new windscreen.

The replacement took much longer than predicted and by then, my parents and I had started to enjoy the delights of Cromwell and Bannockburn, and through to Queensbury, Luggate and Wānaka.

We enjoyed it so much Cromwell became our camping destination for the next few years. Cromwell and Bannockburn is where I had my first trip on wild thyme. It cleared my senses like nothing else. And still does.

Every time I return to the heart of Central Otago the earth moves me, like nowhere else — the soft pastel blue of the Big Sky that changes as the sun rolls across the horizon.

But it is different to the Central I was first introduced to, growing up. In those days there was no Clyde Dam and the Cromwell Gorge was the Grand Canyon of New Zealand, with the best apricot orchards in the country. Cromwell was the closest New Zealand had to a Wild West town. But sadly all that has been lost under Lake Dunstan, formed after the completion of the Clyde Dam in 1993. Construction of the dam was controversial and changed the area for ever. Geological problems during its construction, and the expense of stabilising the gorge walls meant this was the last of Prime Minister Muldoon's Think Big projects.

Although the Clyde Dam did not have universal backing, Lake Dunstan has become a major recreational asset for the area.

❛Every time I return to the heart of Central Otago the earth moves me, like nowhere else — the soft pastel blue of the Big Sky that changes as the sun rolls across the horizon.❜

It adds to the wonderful natural assets of lakes and rivers nearby that make Central Otago so special for outdoor pursuits. The magnificent orchards still grow the best cherries, apricots and other fruit. And the explosion of vineyards has added a new dimension to Central as home to world-class Pinot Noir. A few years ago my mother said when we first went to Cromwell and out to Bannockburn it was as though the hills were moving, with thousands of rabbits on the run. Now the hills are covered in vineyards and grapes that include world-class cafes and restaurants.

So many things have changed. But one thing remains as it was back in the 1950s. The wonderful haunting smell, of wild thyme.

Peter Montgomery is of that rare breed . . . a broadcaster who is better known than most of the sportsmen and women whose deeds he describes. As the voice of New Zealand yachting for more than four decades, Peter Montgomery has covered all the major events including 11 America's Cups, nine Olympic Games and all 12 Whitbread/Volvo races. Peter is recognised as an authority on the sport. His skill and commitment have been recognised across the world. He has regularly commentated in other countries. Peter has been honoured with too many professional awards to list here as well as receiving an MBE in the Queen's Birthday Honours in 1995. His abilities have not been confined to commentating sailing. He has also been a successful sports broadcaster with other sports, including a long stint as a member of the Radio Rugby Team in Auckland.

Peter Montgomery with son Johnny at Mount Difficulty.

Kokonga: seen through a youthful lens.

Jeremy Corbett

Kokonga

As the self-confessed chairman of the shallow club, I'm as surprised as you are that there is a place close to my heart. Though great places are easy to find, locating my heart can prove difficult.

But the place is there. Has been for years, sitting tucked under my right ventricle. The publisher of this book stirred it from its rest and brought its memories pumping back through my arteries.

A magical place from my childhood, probably at the peak of its powers for me when I was 11 or 12, back in the 20th century.

Kokonga. Central Otago. Circa 1970-mumble.

It was where my mum grew up, where Grandma still lived, but most importantly it was Uncle David's farm.

Although I remember experiencing the brilliant stillness of the hoar frost, the fascination at standing on a frozen pond and ice skating/face-planting at nearby Naseby, normally our family would visit during the summer school holidays. It was a long trip and perhaps part of Kokonga's magic to me was the other-worldliness of the place given the tortuous journey to get there.

We lived in Palmerston North, which I guess may also have contributed to the wonderment at anywhere else. Our family of six would squeeze into a Morris 1800 and spend days making the drive / ferry / drive / drive / drive via Christchurch and, crazily now that I look at a map, Dunedin to finally arrive at the best place on earth: Uncle David's farm.

My perception of time and distance was not well developed back then, but I knew when we left Dunedin it would be mere hours before we got there. Slowly the landscape would change and as the hills browned and rounded off I would stir from my travel slumber. The last few corners I knew, and like a dog sniffing home after a long drive I would have my head out the window: alert, excited and animated.

Familiar landmarks, Uncle Ian's postbox, the haystack! Grandma's house, then the driveway, tall trees, rat-a-tat over the cow stop, curving upward past the lip we used for motorbike jumps then turning and pulling to a stop outside the farmhouse, the engine noise replaced by chorus cicadas.

My brothers and I would attempt to spring from the car but would instead stumble out in the way a body does after being cramped in a cocoon for two hours. Then we'd dutifully conduct the hellos and pleasantries before racing out to explore our favourite haunts: the outside room, the lead-lined coloured glass on the outside toilet (I knowww), the tractor shed, the chooks and that other building that had fallen into disrepair. All touchstones that we were truly there.

Over the glorious, sun-filled days that followed, we would tick off all the major attractions and rides: the

> **'Over the glorious, sun-filled days that followed, we would tick off all the major attractions and rides: the 125cc Honda motorbike, smoko, rounding up the sheep, smoko...'**

125cc Honda motorbike, smoko, rounding up the sheep, smoko and the real favourite: feeding out the hay from the flatbed truck before smoko. We'd take turns "driving", as Uncle David stood on the back throwing the bales to the sheep wobbling and jogging up behind.

I asked him one day what he did when we were not there to steer for him. To my horror he told me that he let the truck drive itself while he dispensed the food. The potential disastrous outcomes for my uncle caused me undue worry for months.

He was a favoured uncle not only because of his carefree, swashfarming ways, but also because he extended the same loose boundaries to us kids, always with a sense of humour. Oh, the fits of suppressed giggles as he allowed our older brother, Greg, a puff on a cigarette. Unbeknownst to my brother, we had replaced all of the nicotine with hay. I'm not sure what reaction we were expecting, but not being overly familiar with real cigarettes, Greg merely accepted that this was how they must taste.

We all laughed. An adult condoning the forbidden! Such naughtiness.

The haystack! Always a highlight: It was a lengthy run through a large paddock to get to it, but we'd spend hours in that massive open shed with our cousins; running, laughing, climbing, building forts from bales, endlessly talking nonsense and never, in spite of accepted wisdom, having it end in tears.

Of course it is people that make any place special, and that was true of Kokonga, but when the people weren't around, it still had some sort of hold on me. Out in a paddock alone, leaning on a fence among the brilliantly sunny stillness, gazing at those golden hills bubbling out of the plains in the distance. I'm not equipped to explain it, but all of my senses were engaged and there was a real feeling of connecting. That's a pathetic attempt.

The paintings of Grahame Sydney come closest to capturing it for me. An isolation, but a nourishing one. Whatever it's called, I found it special. I tried to hold onto that feeling by taking a photo. The lens caught just enough to trigger the feeling in someone who had also stood there. I showed it to my mother months later and I could tell that she was transported back. Felt the emotion. She had been chopping onions, so I concede my photo may not have been wholly responsible.

I have not since experienced a sadness over departing like I did when we left that place. The days we spent there evaporated in that hot Central Otago summer. It was definitely my fondness for my uncle, but also a fondness for the place and a heart-breaking knowledge that it would take so much travel and be so long before I would return. I cried when we drove away. The melancholy so deep that it would last way beyond the first ice cream.

A week after we had visited I wrote my uncle a letter in which I said I wished I was there to steer the truck and pleaded for him to be safe and not fall off the back. This brought much good-natured laughter from my parents and I'm sure my uncle.

But God, I meant it.

Jeremy Corbett, 188cm of raw flab with glasses, was once called one of the godfathers of New Zealand stand-up comedy. The speaker was a younger comedian who meant it as an insult. Comedian, radio and TV presenter, computer programmer and Leo, he was born in Westport, grew up in Palmerston North and now lives in Auckland with his wife, Megan, two beautiful daughters Charlie and Billie and a golden retriever called Nugget. He hosts 7DAYS on TV3. Most of his success has come from just sticking around.

Jeremy Corbett (right) with various young relations.

Gore: equal opportunity hometown.

Mike Puru

Gore

For years it has been ridiculed as the gay capital of New Zealand, following a visit from Newsboy and Havoc where they mocked the town for being homophobic. Ironically I am gay and from Gore, but it's far from homophobic. It's home to some of the best memories I have.

I lived on the outskirts of Gore — a predominantly farming community but also home to a huge meatworks where both my parents worked.

The reason I loved my time there is simple. No distractions, from the fast-moving lifestyle that city kids experience, and a population that was big enough to stimulate opportunities but small enough to allow anyone of any age to participate because numbers were needed.

I lived first in a small township called Waikoikoi, where I attended the local primary school with a roll of around 25 pupils and found it more like hanging out with family friends. We had access to an outdoor pool for a fee of $10 a year, which paid for the key to the padlocked gate that you could easily just jump.

I loved helping the farming neighbour feed out in the snow and grub thistles, and when our house burnt to the ground at age nine the community rallied around my very young parents (26-ish) and provided a house and enough TVs and furniture for about five families. It was quite overwhelming for a young boy to witness — it taught me a lot about humanity.

We moved to another small township outside of Gore, called Pukerau, to rebuild our lives and I ended up getting a paper round — fourteen newspapers, all about one kilometre apart, down dusty gravel roads where dead lambs were piled up like rubbish at the end of long driveways, but it gave me a sense of freedom and responsibility in my early years. I saved my $12 a week and decided to buy a 10-speed. It was flash, with skinny wheels, gears and a tremendous paint job, but a foolish move as it was no good on the gravel rounds, so I eventually bought a scooter. Where else at age 13 could you do a paper round on a motorbike?

I also worked in a petrol station in Pukerau during the weekends. A whole day from 7am to 7pm where local farmers would buy ice creams and smokes and we would mark it down as "farm supplies". I learnt quickly how to converse with adults and gained respect from the locals who were mainly white.

The Māori population was tiny in Southland but I never thought about race and the stereotypes that could have been floating around — I was just a local kid. There wasn't much culture around. I was one of three Māori in the secondary school of 320, so never embraced my heritage. I can remember the small local marae, which was a basic corrugated iron shed painted in that deep brown red colour synonymous with marae, but was hardly ever in use.

It was mainly employed as a 21st venue and often as the base for the local dog shows where I used to

> **'One thing about being so sheltered from race is the fact you don't ever think about society's perceptions and that certainly helped me just give everything a go in Gore.'**

sell K-bars and fizzy for Mum as she was heavily involved in showing off her German shepherds. I wish there were more Māori around when I was young. As a broadcaster I sometimes feel I failed my ancestors. I hardly know how to do the haka and my French partner knows more te reo than I do, which is embarrassing. But it's never too late.

One thing about being so sheltered from race is the fact you don't ever think about society's perceptions and that certainly helped me just give everything a go in Gore.

The town had a thriving operatic scene and I helped build and renovate the theatre which we performed in and where I now stand as a host of major Gore events. I worked in a local music shop on a Friday night selling CDs (mainly The Dudes and country music) and was probably one of the first people in Gore to use a cell phone to order stock from Auckland. It was cheaper back then to use the cellphone than to use a landline, but the exhilaration of talking and walking down the street at the same time was ego-stroking at its best.

That's the beauty of Gore and its people — everyone knows each other — everyone had a vested interest in each other and it was a community in its true sense. Doors were never locked, milk came straight from a cow and credit cards were only used if you couldn't barter your way to a car repair. It was the type of place where you swapped some paua from the Catlins with the road grader and he would do your driveway so it was pothole-free for another three months.

I owe a lot to Gore. The local radio station was only live for four hours a day, and once I had completed some work experience I ended up filling in on the breakfast show at the tender, inexperienced age of 17. Here I was pumping gas on the weekend, working the music store on a Friday night and filling in on breakfast radio, before I raced to school where I was head boy. I was sticking my fingers in as many pies as I could, like a baby with playdough — experiencing grown up stuff and being shielded from sex, drugs and rock 'n' roll. It was the sort of innocence that smacks you in the face hard when you leave for the big smoke, but also the innocence that allows you to grow at the right pace, and that's what makes Gore special to me.

Beautiful, deep green-grassed farmland that requires no filter — rugged untouched coastline only a short drive away, where trees bend like ballerinas and, no matter where you are, a deep fresh air — so unique it's the first thing you notice when you get home.

Every year over Queen's Birthday weekend Gore motel owners blew the dust off the "No" sign and slid it happily in front of the vacancy sign as motels filled up. it was time for Gore to come alive and host the annual Gold Guitars — a huge country music festival over three days that filled the town with tassels and cowboy hats. The first year Mum took me to see the battle of amateur singers, there was an international guest — Freddy Fender. I didn't care much for him but was fascinated by the throng of TV cameras and reporters crawling over Gore. With pride I would get so excited when *One News* did a report on the Gold Guitars — it gave a taste of fame, and the idea that telling all of New Zealand what was happening in sleepy Gore seemed a fun job. Maybe that's what led me to broadcasting — Hell, even Maggie Barry filmed a *Heartland* episode here, and I remember standing fascinated as a small TV crew filmed down Main Street — it was just so damn exciting for me!

And not only the capital of New Zealand's country music scene, but also of Romney sheep breeding, and the world capital of brown trout fishing, all proudly trumpeted through a series of sculptures and statues that sit proudly in Main Street. But it's also my capital of genuine people. There to help you grow, young families wanting the best for their kids or fourth-generation farmers keeping the economy alive.

I owe a lot to you, Gore. I have an incredible life and although I am gay and was once worried your stigma would be amplified by having a TV and radio personality flying your flag, I fly it proudly knowing that you created it . You were big enough to give me the chances and small enough to let me try anything, and I'm truly grateful.

Mike Puru is a TV and radio presenter who spent 20 years at The Edge radio station where he won the Sir Paul Holmes Broadcaster of the Year Award for 2014 with Jay Jay and Dom and the Best Breakfast Show Award 2014 and 2016 at the New Zealand Radio Awards. He is currently the host of The Bachelor New Zealand *and TV3's The Cafe as well as a guest presenter on Radio Live. Mike is also a presenter on Yes Shop, broadcast in New Zealand and Australia.*

Mike Puru and family shortly after their house was destroyed by fire.

Rakiura/Stewart Island: boardwalk at Mason Bay.

Brian Parkinson

Stewart Island

I first went to Stewart Island in the late 1980s and this involved a four-day trip by bus, train and boat from my home in the Bay of Plenty. Oban the main settlement of Stewart was, then, a small settlement consisting of a pub, a school, and a general store along with facilities to service the fleet of fishing boats. Visitors, then, consisted of trampers along with a small number of naturalists, generally referred to by the locals as bunny huggers. Most evenings the fishermen retired to the pub which claims to be the world's most southerly. (It's not.) And here they spent their time telling tall stories to the visitors.

Behind the pub a paradise duck lurked and one of its favourite activities was to dash out and peck passing schoolchildren on their butts. Presumably they got to school a lot sooner. It was a source of some amusement to local residents, but not so much to the kids.

The trampers mostly consisted of Teutonic types who were looking for tracks that were less congested than those of the South Island and had decided to walk the island's North-West Circuit Track. This is about 125 km long and even the very fit took more than a week to walk it .This was generally likened to spending a very long time tramping through a mosquito-infested swamp. However, this is perhaps a little unkind; it should more charitably be called a sandfly-infested swamp. Trampers on Stewart Island are easily distinguished by their large boots, short shorts and testosterone-charged demeanour. And the guys are even worse.

The naturalists generally took shorter walks around Oban as this was the only settlement in New Zealand where they could see a number of our rarer native birds without getting too wet and muddy. Kākā, kererū and tūī could usually be seen flying overhead in Oban and on a leisurely stroll you can easily spot smaller birds such as tomtits and fantails along with other species, generally known as LBJs — Little Brown Jobs. Actually if you took your meals outside, there was a very good chance a kākā would join you. Ulva Island was just a short boat trip offshore and here there were quite a lot of birds, most obviously weka, which if given the opportunity, would happily share your lunch, shamelessly disregarding the "Do Not Feed the Weka" signs.

When the gum trees along the road to Acker's Point are fruiting, kākā gorge on the gum nuts and can get seriously discombobulated. Like a lot of drunks they can get very noisy and overly familiar. Also, their flying becomes very erratic, often resulting in spectacular collisions with trees and telegraph poles. On my first visit I stayed in the Oban Caravan Park which has been regrettably long closed. Caravans have wonderful acoustics but having a gang of kākā carousing and hooning about on your roof for the fourth or fifth early morning in a row, causes dawn choruses to lose a lot of their charm, especially as dawn in summer on Stewart Island, is around 3 a.m. I suspect that this is where the expression "as pissed as a parrot" originates.

> **'When the gum trees along the road to Acker's Point are fruiting, kākā gorge on the gum nuts and can get seriously discombobulated. Like a lot of drunks they can get very noisy and overly familiar.'**

On Stewart Island you probably have the best chance of seeing kiwi anywhere, as here, because of the shortened nights in summer, they are forced to forage during the day. There are some on Ulva, and you stand a good chance of seeing them away from the main settlement, particularly in places like Mason Bay. I saw a couple there at about 3 o'clock in the afternoon.

For the seabird enthusiast Stewart Island is one of the best places in the world to go. Three species of penguin — the Fiordland crested, the yellow-eyed and the little blue can sometimes be seen, particularly around Ulva Island and if you take a stroll out to Acker's Point in the evening, to watch the shearwaters arriving at their nesting sites, you can hear the penguins in their rafts offshore chattering to each other, presumably discussing matters piscine, and waiting for darkness before coming ashore and around dusk you have a good chance of meeting little blue penguins on their way to their nests. They are fairly relaxed and after glaring at you suspiciously, they waddle off into the scrub to their nests. These nests are usually distinguished by their pong as they are surrounded by regurgitated fish and penguin droppings and this is why bach-owners, which on Stewart Island are called cribs, are very reluctant proprietors, when penguins nest under their floor boards. The yellow-eyed penguins have diminished in numbers in recent years but are still hanging on and if you don't see any on Stewart Island, you should try the Catlins. If looking for penguins remember to give them plenty of space as they are easily spooked.

For the larger seabirds you need to go offshore. I was fortunate enough to have a fisherman friend who took me out while he was crayfishing, so managed to see a number of the smaller albatrosses, among them Buller's, black-browed and shy mollymawks, along with a variety of shearwaters and petrels. If you are keen to see these birds pelagic trips can be arranged for those interested, so ask at the Department of Conservation office for a list of operators.

It is an unhappy fact that mollymawks and their larger kin, the albatrosses, need strong winds to fly efficiently, so the stronger the winds, the more chance you have of seeing them, and the less likely you are to appreciate them. Anyway when you are back ashore, you can take solace in the old saw which says the best cure for sea sickness is to find a tree and sit under it, and Stewart Island has some beautiful trees. On one trip to Bluff, when the seas were particularly rough, I met an American lady who had been told that crossing Foveaux Strait on the ferry provided the best chance to see albatrosses and mollymawks. Half-way through the trip, I spotted a mollymawk which I helpfully pointed out to the lady who by this time was turning a rather fetching shade of green, only to be told "I couldn't give a shit".

In the 30 years I have been going there Stewart Island has gone through drastic changes.

With the introduction of fishing quotas small fishermen have now largely disappeared and the gazetting of the Rakiura National Park has meant that Stewart Island is now mostly devoted with varying degrees of enthusiasm to tourism.

In summer, Oban has a significant flow of tourists and the local homestays and lodges put up their prices at this time of year, to take advantage of this. Cheaper accommodation can be found but this is often some distance out of Oban, but a walk of six kilometres to get a cup of coffee, soon looses its charm.

A trip to Ulva Island to see its birds is a must. However, Ulva gets a bit congested at this time and this is where we can talk about "twitchers". Twitchers are a group of bird-watching enthusiasts who want to see as many species of birds as they can during their lifetimes and each new bird is called a twitch. They are sometimes encountered in god-forsaken places around the world looking for a lesser-spotted what not. To get a twitch, they look at the bird through their binoculars for a millisecond, then completely lose interest in it and dash off to twitch the next one. They can easily be identified by their large binoculars, assorted cameras and note-books and their obsessive-compulsive behaviour. Ulva has ten or twelve twitchable birds, so in summer there are a lot of twitchers there. Be warned, even if you don't get trampled underfoot, they are quite likely to bore you to death.

The beautiful New Zealand sea lion often hauls out on Ulva beaches for a snooze and some visitors have a strange urge to have their pictures taken next to them. Sea lions have long teeth and short fuses and have no wish at all to be included in your selfie. Although, I suppose this provides a very good chance, for the interested observer, to see natural selection in action.

Nowadays, birds are not so common but can still be seen in reasonable numbers. On my most recent visit, kākā were around my homestay most times of the day, but I suspect there was some sort of bribery involved. I went, as per usual to Ulva and this was the first time I didn't see a weka there, although I did hear a couple — maybe they were waiting for a break in the traffic. Perhaps outside the tourist season is best.

Brian Parkinson is a naturalist and writer. He has written more than 20 books and discovered some "30 or 40" species of flora and fauna, many of which have been named for him.

Brian Parkinson encounters a Lyall's daisy near the top of the Tin Range.

Moana Maniapoto

The Ocean

Ko au te moana, ko te moana ko au.
I am the Ocean, the Ocean is me.

Ocean — that giant mirror under a blue sky, that dark and furious mass scowling up at concrete clouds. Ocean is my landscape.

When we were kids, our father would drive his brood out from Invercargill to Oreti Beach.

With buckets in hand, we would tear across the sands, spreading out in search of a tiny, tell-tale bubble on the surface. Then we would kick our heel into that sweet spot and twist it this way and that, until the reveal. Yes. There lay the pearly white shell, its meaty tongue protruding as if in mid-haka. We'd carry our precious cargo back to the breakers, give it a quick wash and drop it gently into our bucket, all under the watchful eye of our father.

There is no more toheroa gathering on Ōreti Beach. And I'm no longer knee-high-to-a-grasshopper.

My name is Moana. It means ocean in Māori. Can't say I ever thought about it, really. And then one day, while my band and I were touring Europe, we were threatened with a lawsuit after releasing my self-named album into Germany. I had breached a trademark on the word Moana. There was nothing I could do but keep calm and carry on. Even my audiences thought it was ridiculous that a foreign company could control the use of a Polynesian word.

Ocean has inspired much of my songwriting because Ocean carries her own tales. The proverb above says much about the relationship between humans and Ocean. Polynesian scholar Epeli Hau'ofa said that for Polynesians, we are connected rather than separated by the sea. And that we should not be defined by the smallness of our islands, but by the greatness of our oceans. Such a powerful way of looking at the world.

All New Zealanders are descended from saltwater

people. My mother's grandparents sailed from Ireland and England. My dad traced his whakapapa back fourteen generations to those who sailed from Hawaiki. Their journey, the names of those who travelled, encounters along the way, even some of the incantations, are still recounted on the marae.

Tama-te-kapua was the captain of the Te Arawa voyaging canoe, Ngātoro-i-rangi, the spiritual leader and navigator.

The captain had a roving eye. As the giant waka sailed from Hawaiki to Aotearoa, he attempted to seduce Keaora, the wife of Ngātoro-i-rangi. The tohunga wasn't impressed. He recited an incantation to call up a taniwha known as Te Korokoro o te Parata. The seas grew rough, threatening to swallow Te Arawa. Only the protestations of his wife and frightened crew caused Ngātoro-i-rangi to calm the waters. When the waka eventually landed in Aotearoa, Tama-te-Kapua had fisticuffs with another leader whose wife he seduced. Rangitoto Island was named because Tama-te-Kapua ended up with a bloody nose. The full name is Te-Rangi-i-toto-ai-te-ihu-o-Tamatekapua.

THE OLD MAN of the Sea sat at my dining room table one Matariki, a glass of ruby red held precariously in one hand. Hekenukumai Busby is a waka builder. Almost every waka on display at Waitangi every Waitangi Day was built by him. Hec can see the finished waka as he gazes at a tree in the forest. I've seen him take a huge log on the island of Maui and, in a week, reveal a waka that none of us, not even other master carvers could see.

Hec is also a master of the art of celestial navigation, taught to him by Mau Pialug, a Micronesian who helped Hawaiians and Māori revive the tradition lost to the Polynesians.

I asked Hec if in his voyages around the Pacific, he had ever seen or heard of this taniwha, Te Korokoro o te Parata. He thought about it and then his eyes lit up.

"There's a place near the Kermadec trench," he said. "All the little fish converge and they swim and swim and it creates, like, a whirlpool. And that's where the whales come to feed while they're on their big journey." Te Korokoro o te Parata — the Throat of Te Parata.

EVERY NIGHT I hear waves from my bed. When I walk into my home, the sea fills my view. There are moments when aquas, greens and blues streak upwards and outwards to the horizon. I love the sight, the smell and spirit of Ocean. It's intoxicating but I find it frightening. After all my iwi are fresh-water people from Rotorua and Taupo.

My name may be Moana. But I couldn't do what Hec, Jack Thatcher or Hoturoa Barclay-Kerr do. They sail for weeks on Ocean, no land in sight, guided by the stars. How do you do that, I ask? They shrug. They know what they are doing, they know it's been done before, they have gods and ancestors with them. They aren't doing it by themselves.

IT TOOK ABOUT 70 minutes to compose "Not Alone", my favourite song on the album *RIMA*.

I wrote it on the drive from Muriwai to Piha, inspired by footage of those voyagers out in the elements. Whenever a line came to mind, I'd pull over and record it by singing into my phone. And then Scotty Morrison channelled those ancestral navigators to write and record the kind of karakia they would have chanted before those big voyages. It's hypnotic, soothing. It calms the senses.

"Not Alone" celebrates ancient voyages and these modern-day navigators. Generations apart, they possess both courage and a sense of adventure. It's all about connection: the past to the present, the spiritual world to the human world and to each other.

Here is the rest of my love letter to Ocean and those who seek to move through her into the unknown. It's also for anyone navigating challenges in their personal lives.

Moana Maniapoto graduated from Auckland University Faculty of Law but is best known as a singer, songwriter, documentary maker and champion of indigenous causes.

Not Alone

I've come so far
Journey's been long
Searching for something
A place to belong
Wind and the waves
Carried me here
Hope can move mountains
Faith destroy fear

I'm not alone
I'm coming home

Wide, open space
Promise of land
Pull of tomorrow
Sense that I can
I may be tempted
No turning back
Something keeps burning,
burning, burning
I understand

I'm not alone
I'm coming home

I hear the pitter-patter
Does it matter?
Heart is breaking, no mistaking
Bitter love, sky above
This is what we're made of.
Eyes wide open, full of hope and
Tired of waiting
Contemplating
Take my hand
Understand
I know nothing

I'm not alone
I'm coming home

Moana Maniapoto and her namesake.

Acknowledgments

Thanks firstly to all those who have contributed to this book, and Forest and Bird for their support. A special word of appreciation to all those mums, dads, aunts, uncles and siblings who sorted through basements, old suitcases and long-unopened drawers to provide pictures of the contributors.

Picture Credits

Title page and pages 29, 40, 45, 52, 56, 60, 63, 64, 67, 69, 72, 76, 80, 88, 114, 166, 208 Stephen Entwisle.

All other images by Oneshot except:
11 The Video Factory; 15 courtesy Suzy Cato; 19 Anika Moa; 20 and 23 courtesy Dame Gillian Whitehead; 24 and 27 Photos courtesy Dr Jason Smith; 31 courtesy Suzanne Lynch; 32 and 35 Cedric Nissen; 39 courtesy Penny Whiting; 42 Jaimie Webster Haines; 47 Chris Bailey; 48 Suzanne McFadden; 51 Eugene Bingham; 55 B. Cornish; 59 courtesy Tricia Scott; 66 courtesy Kevin Roberts; 71 courtesy Mai Chen; 74 courtesy Robert Sullivan; 79 courtesy Joan Withers; 83 courtesy Lynda Hallinan; 87 Peter Bush; 91 John Savage; 92 Eve Holmes; 95 courtesy Vaughan Smith; 99 courtesy Scotty Morrison; 103 Nick Malmholt; 109 Ita Belic; 113 courtesy Aroha Awarau; 116 courtesy Debbie Harwood; 121 courtesy Jenny Pattrick; 122 and 125 courtesy Donald Kerr; 129 courtesy Karl Maughan; 133 courtesy Kerry Fox; 137 courtesy Chris Bourke; 141 courtesy Alexis Pritchard; 142 and 145 Max Walker; 146 Conrad Armstrong; 149 Kitchin family collection; 150 courtesy Erica Crawford; 153 Faanati Mamea; 154 Mandy Reid; 157 Richard Broad; 161 courtesy Kate De Goldi; 162 and 165 Andy Currie; 169 courtesy Jack Tame; 170 Steve Attwood; 173 courtesy Paula Ryan; 177 courtesy Jane Bowron; 178 photograph courtesy of Otago Daily Times 181 courtesy Fiona Farrell; 182 and 185 Brando Yelavich; 188 courtesy Murray Crane; 190 Steve Attwood; 193 courtesy Jordan Luck; 199 courtesy Jo Seagar; 203 courtesy Jodi Brown; 204 Brian High; 207 Geoff Mackley; 210 courtesy Peter Montgomery; 212 Jeremy Corbett; 215 Corbett family collection; 219 courtesy Mike Puru; 223 courtesy Brian Parkinson; 227 courtesy Moana Maniapoto.

Index of People & Places